AF478370

THE JAGUAR DRIVER'S YEAR BOOK 1978

compiled by *Paul Skilleter*

THE
MAGPIE
PUBLISHING
COMPANY

THE
MAGPIE
PUBLISHING
COMPANY

Printed in Great Britain by
Ernest G. Bond Limited, 2-6 Victoria
Way, Charlton, London SE7, for
The Magpie Publishing Company
'Holmerise' Seven Hills Road
Cobham, Surrey.
(Also at 5 Rectory Road, Beckenham, Kent)
Case-bound by Papworth Industries,
Papworth Everard, Cambridge.

ISBN 0 906234 02 6

© 1979

Acknowledgements

This book would have been almost impossible to produce without the help of many Jaguar enthusiasts who supplied photographs of cars and events. We cannot name them all, but would particularly like to thank the following — Mike Beales of Sussex who provided tremendous coverage of many JDC events, John Williams, S-type Register Secretary, whose professional prints were a delight, Stuart Sadd who again provided the professional's touch, Rich Zolla of the Classic Jaguar Association (USA) who supplied a superb variety of SS and Jaguar pictures taken in the States, Claus Rossin and Karen Miller of the Empire Division, JCNA, who both sent large quantities of picture illustrating East Coast Jaguar activities, and lastly our own incredibly hard-working club chairman David Harvey, who somehow found time to cover Scottish Jaguar Day and East Anglian Day.

NB: Pictures not credited in captions were in most cases taken by Paul Skilleter.

Contents

Introduction

This is the second Jaguar Driver's Year Book, and its contents have been much expanded over last year's edition. The Year Book now includes the most comprehensive listing of services and parts sources for obsolete Jaguars published in this country, and, marking that car's rapidly rising popularity, the most detailed investigation ever into 'E' type bodywork maintenance.

The informative listings of Jaguar cars now includes much additional data (such as production figures), and this year is accompanied by a picture of virtually every single type of Jaguar made, to make this a valuable reference and identification aid.

And, of course, the Year Book maintains its lavish coverage of club and Jaguar events, with many pictures of Jaguars from all over the world. The vast majority have never been published before, and we hope that it will provide many hours of enjoyable browsing.

PAUL SKILLETER,
DECEMBER 1978

About The Jaguar Drivers Club

Although the Jaguar isn't a high-production car as such, the club here in Great Britain is one of the largest of its kind, with well over 5,000 members. It all started in 1956, which meant that the JDC celebrated its 21st year in 1977; the club has certainly come a long way in those years.

It would take up far too much space to relate every single thing which the club offers its members, but briefly, there's variety enough for everyone. Owners of obsolete models will most likely be concerned about spare parts and technical advice, and assistance of this sort is achieved mainly through the club's 'registers', whose spares secretaries will endeavour to help members locate sources of supply, and furnish technical information. It costs no extra to belong to a Register, which is covered by the overall subscription of £7.00 annually, and a joining fee of £3.00.

Each register also has a regular news column in the club's monthly magazine, the 'Jaguar Driver'. This is a large (A4 size), professionally produced publication, and it contains features on club events, maintenance and renovation, and Jaguar news from all over the world. The 'classified' advertisement columns also provide lots of interesting reading, with many parts and cars being advertised each month. The 'Jaguar Driver' is posted free to every member.

The club also has what we call 'Area Centres'. These are local groups of members who meet once a month in pubs and various hostelries, and who organise local events — which can range from barbecues, through film evenings, to continental trips. There are about 30 Area Centres within the club, so the chances are there's one near you — a list appears later on, though check with JDC Headquarters to make sure the venue hasn't changed after the appearance of this Year Book.

On a 'national' level, the club organises a good number of meetings, usually featuring a 'concours d'elegance' and held at some picturesque or interesting location which will keep the whole family entertained. Again, these span the country, with Jaguar 'days' occuring as far north as Doune, Scotland, and Beaulieu in the south; as indeed, this Year Book relates. An annual Spares Day is held too, a very popular bring-and-buy occasion which attracts hundreds of people, including many from the continent.

For those with sporting tastes, the JDC holds one of the premier 'Historic' race meetings in the calendar, where the most exotic of sports-racing Jaguars and other cars can be seen competing. Sprint meetings and hill climbs are usually held too.

An important project which will be a focus of attention within the club over the next few years is the newly-launched 'Building Fund', through which the club hopes to purchase its own freehold offices in 1981, the JDC's 25th anniversary year.

Up-to-date information can be supplied and membership enquiries gladly answered by the club HQ, at the Norfolk Hotel, Harrington Road, London SW7 (01-584-9494/5). If you're a Jaguar owner who isn't a member, we look forward to welcoming you into the club very soon.

David Harvey,
Chairman,
Jaguar Driver's Club.

The Club Year

As befits a large motor club with an enthusiastic membership, the JDC organises and takes part in many activities over the year, and over the next few pages we follow the happenings of 1978 in pictures.

The club's 'historic' motor race meeting at Silverstone in March heads the list, and is followed by various events, most of which are organised either by the club's Registers, or its Area Centres. As can be seen, events are held in virtually every part of the country, and certainly the JDC is one of the most 'de-centralised' of motor clubs, thanks largely to its enthusiastic Area Centres.

We look forward to an equally active 1979 season, and invite all those with an interest in Jaguars to come to our meetings — an outline calendar of events will be found elsewhere, and you can check with JDC HQ for up-to-date information on what is planned during the coming year.

EAST MIDLANDS RALLY

Wollaton Park was the scene of the club's first rally of 1978, which was on April 2nd. This was the Nottingham Area Rally organised by the East Midlands Centre whose representative is John Williams; he took the picture.

Distinguished visitor to the East Midland's spring rally was this 1939 SS 100, owned by Mr B.W. Foster. *Photo: John Williams.*

One of the most active of JDC centres, the East Midlands Area boasts many keen members, some owning a variety of Jaguars. This is Rob Saunders, with his Mk I Jaguar saloon, 420, and, in the foreground, XK 140 fixed-head coupe.
Photo: John Williams.

BEAULIEU

A superb line-up of Mk V, and Mk IV drophead and saloon, the concours finalist in the older saloons class, during the club's annual Spring Rally at the National Motor Museum in May.

This very well kept Series 3 V12 E-type came from Holland, and was placed in the 'concours'. Certainly, an increasing number of enthusiasts from abroad now attend JDC rallies, both for the fun of it, and for the purpose of buying spares — hopefully cheaper and more easily than in their own country.

A feature of the Beaulieu meeting is always the activity in the driving test arena, where car and driver are required to perform various manouvres. Obviously the driver of this XK 120 roadster finds it easier to leap over the XK's low door than open it — though he appears to have left the car in the conventional way, judging from the other open door.
Photo: Mike Beales.

Mr Brumitt's 4.2 E-type lines up for a cup-snatching session, brake lights on and puff of smoke from the exhaust.
Photo: Mike Beales.

One exercise at Beaulieu required the competitor to swop plastic cups about, which is what Mike Cooper (of Brickmaker's Arms fame) is doing here before leaping back into his V12 E-type.
Photo: Mike Beales.

JDC GOODWOOD

On June 11th, the club held its Sprint Meeting at the famous old Goodwood racing circuit — now alas, demoted to testing and sprints only, as the safety aspects of the course don't match up to modern requirements. Here Keith Webber's standard Mk II saloon, sun-roof open, swerves through the chicane.   *Photo: Mike Beales.*

John Simms, XK Register secretary, demonstrating that the day of the sprint was blessed with good weather. His son is obviously interested in Dad's E-type, which was originally modified by Dick Protheroe.   *Photo: Mike Beales.*

The Simms' E-type at full chat out of the chicane and on the way to a class win.
Photo: Mike Beales.

Other E-type drivers didn't have such good luck — Peter Griffiths explains what went wrong with his Series 2 (which was a ruined clutch).
Photo: Mike Beales.

No such maladies bothered Peter Trent, judging by his cheerful look as he changes a plug on his 2.4 'classic saloon'.
Photo: Mike Beales.

JDC activity in the north of England has not always been great, but recently, thanks to the hard work of a number of faithful Jaguar owners, things have really blossomed and now Yorkshire Jaguar Day is a regular event. For 1978, it was held at Nostell Priory, and over 100 Jaguars arrived to celebrate the occasion — this picture, by George Pexton, shows just some of them.

'E' TYPE DAY

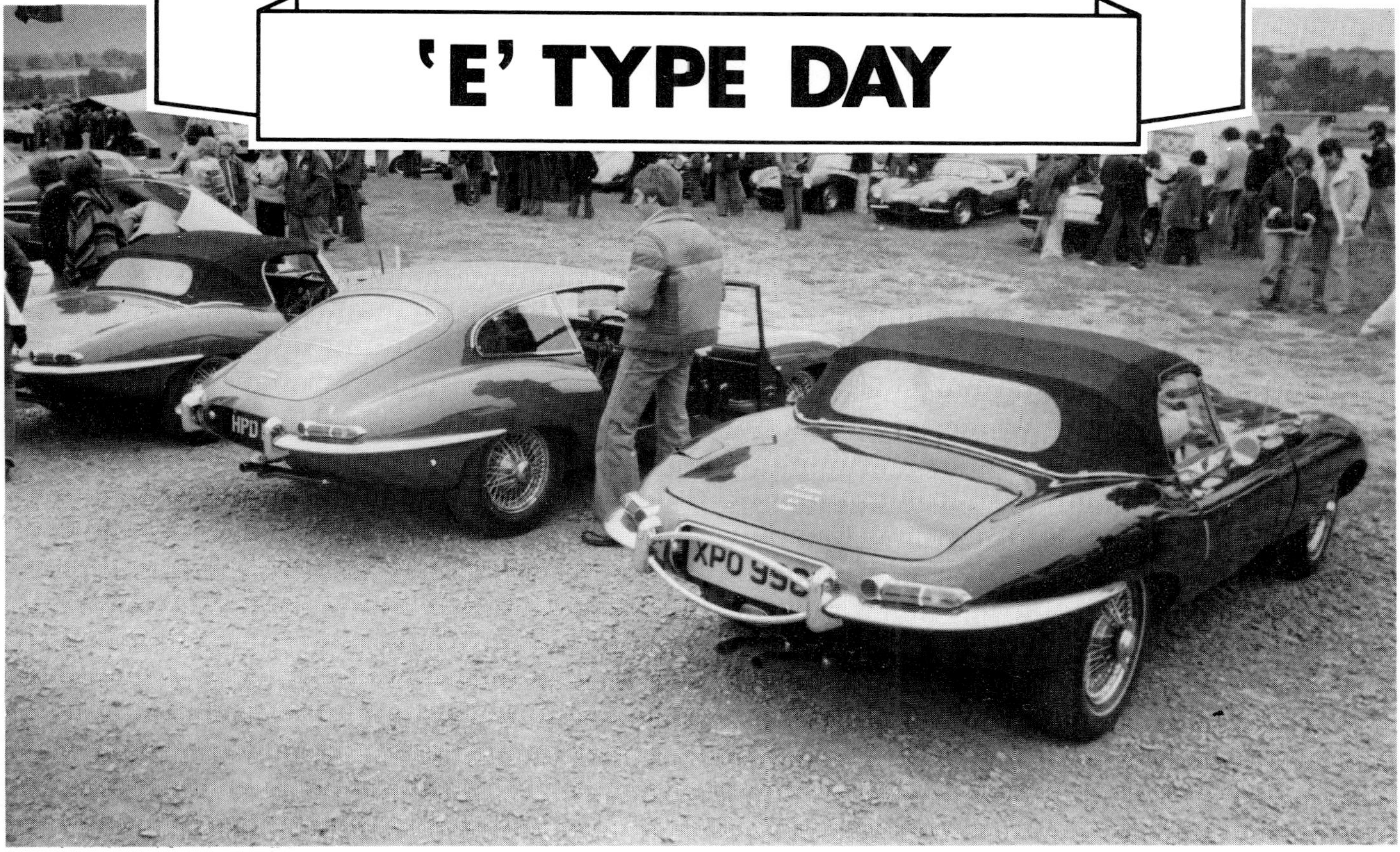

With the rapid rise in 'E' type Register membership, it wasn't surprising that International 'E' type Day turned out to be one of the biggest club events of the year. 'E' types of all sorts were represented, and some of the concours entrants can be seen in the foreground.

Not just standard 'E' types were present — both the Guyson 'E' types came; these are Series 3 cars with new outer bodywork in glass fibre, designed by Bill Towns, who also created the current Aston Martin V8 shape. Note the number plate — the Guyson bead-blasting concern sponsored the project. Bryan Corser's beautiful XKSS is seen behind the 'E'.

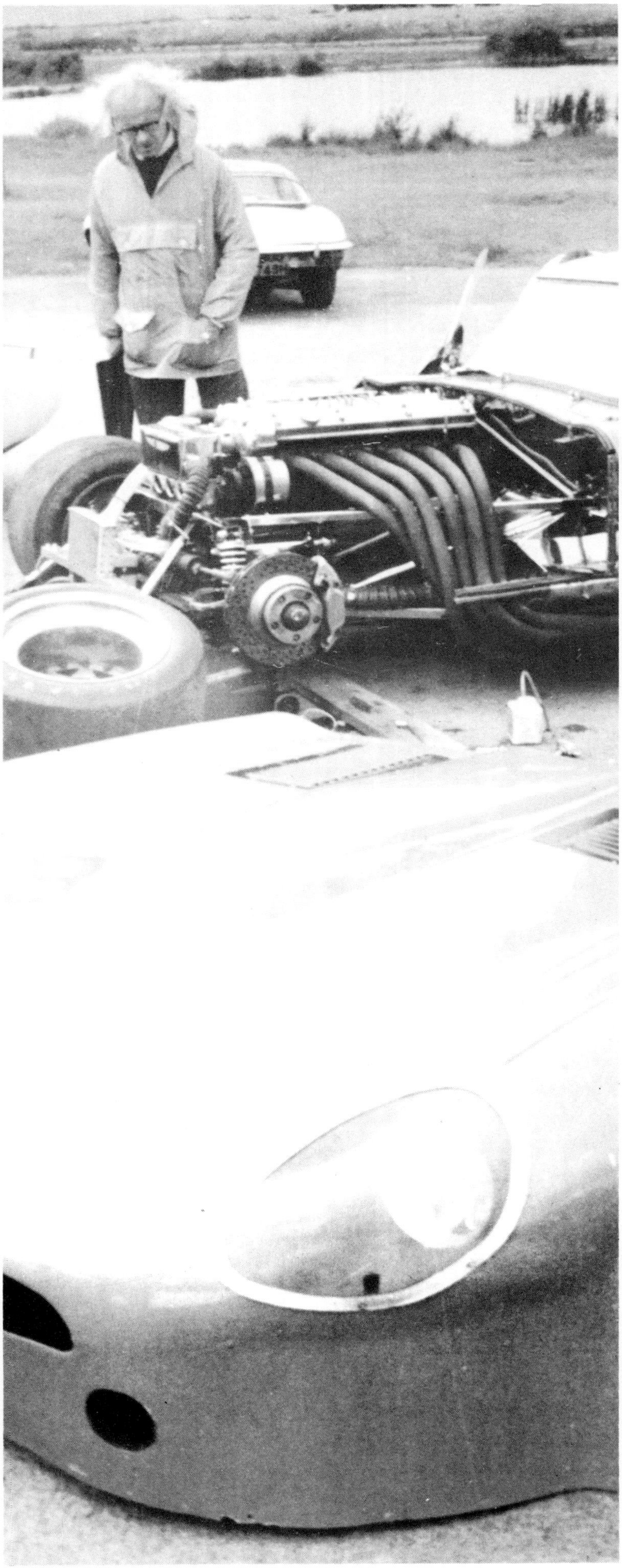

'E' type Day, held on June 25th, used the Mallory Park racing circuit as its venue, and took advantage of the fact by opening the circuit for a test-session; mostly members with road 'E' types used the facility, but some mod-sports cars came as well — here is a highly modified example receiving attention to its brakes.

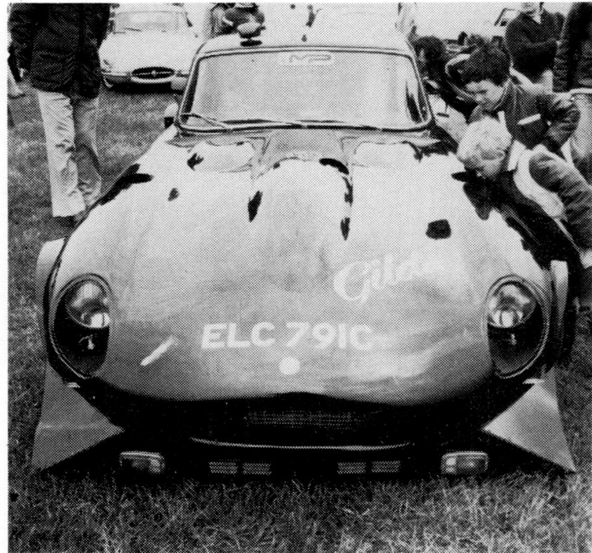

This is 'Gilda'. We don't know much about her, but she certainly attracted attention at 'E' type Day. She is a little different from the ordinary 'E' type. . .

Gilda from behind. Truncated tail incorporates a spoiler which is part of the rear door. Very wide (10-inch) wheels are fitted, plus a side exhaust, suitably protected by wire mesh. All very nicely executed, and what a long way to travel from the King's Road.

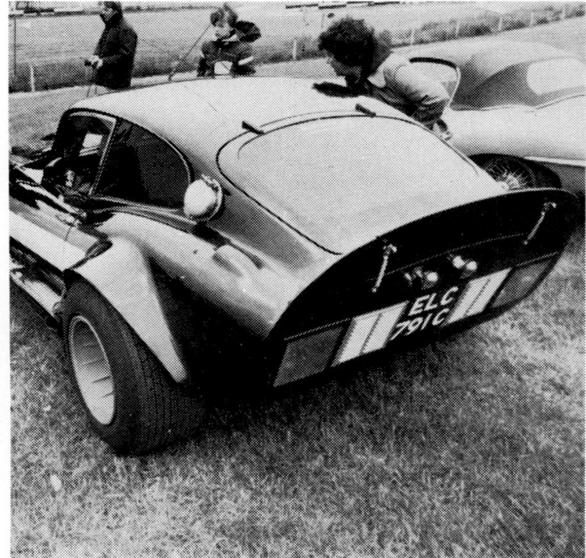

PACKINGTON 'XJ DAY'

Organised by the JDC Midlands Area, the big meeting at Packington Hall near Coventry in July, saw the brand-new XJ Register come into being.

Over 100 XJs supported the launch of the new register, and XJ secretary Rick Reading enrolled something over 70 new XJ Register members in the special marquee.
Photo: Mike Beales.

Packington also saw an autokhana, and while an XJ might not be the most handy of cars for this sort of work, there were plenty of keen tryers as this picture shows! Bill Haigh's XJ6 won the saloon car class in fact, and collected car radio equipment given by Joseph Lucas.
Photo: Mike Beales.

Besides modern Jaguars, a fine display of older cars was on view at Packington, including Jaguar's own S.S.1, John Owen's SS 100, and Bryan Corser's D-type-based XKSS.

A real jaguar! Someone brought along this cub, and needless to say it was a star attraction. A slightly surprised looking club chairman David Harvey holds the 'cat' in this picture.
Photo: Mike Beales.

The S-type Register was also represented at Packington, with John Williams' well-organised HQ ready to answer questions on S-type/420/420G subjects, and to enrol members.

Packington Jaguar Day culminated in a parade of concours and 'special interest' Jaguars; here a Series 3 2-plus-2 heads a convoy up to the Hall.

NATIONAL CLASSIC CAR CONCOURS

The JDC has enjoyed a pretty amazing run of success in concours events during 1978 thanks to the high standard of preparation by JDC members. The National Classic Car Concours, sponsored by Thoroughbred & Classic Cars magazine, is one of the most important of its type in the country, so no wonder that we were delighted when member Bill Athawes's 1965 4.2 'E' type roadster was nominated 'Best Car of the Day'.   *Photo: John Williams.*

Not only that, but a Jaguar also won the Saloon Car Class A, and Gerry Margrave is seen here collecting his silverware with GEA 1, his superlative 420 saloon   *Photo: John Williams*

Moment of decision — concours judge Rodney Leach (well known through his 'Nostalgia' business) takes one last look at Bill's 'E' type, before nominating it for the top award in conjunction with the other judges.

Altogether, the JDC fielded 10 cars at Weston Park, Staffs.. for this big event, and very nearly won the Team Prize too, which would have been the second year running. Our pairing, however, failed on a technicality. For one JDC entrant, it was his first concours — Mr. F.T. Lloyd with his beautifully original Mk 1 Jaguar saloon.   *Photo: John Williams.*

TOWN & COUNTRY FESTIVAL, STONELIEGH

At the huge Motoring Festival at Stoneleigh, car clubs were invited to present stands for judging. This is part of the JDC's display, with the theme 'Sir William Lyons, This is Your Life'.

The earliest exhibit on the stand illustrated how the young William Lyons started in business, when in 1922 with William Walmsley he founded the Swallow Sidecar Company. *Photo: John Williams*

The first Swallow car used the Austin Seven as its basis, and was represented at Stoneleigh by the 1930 saloon from Jaguar's own collection.
Photo: John Williams

Then came the first true S.S. car, in two versions originally, the S.S.1 and S.S.2. This is Mrs Joan Farrell's S.S.2 saloon, well known in JDC circles as concours winner and regular attender at club functions.

The first 'Jaguar' appeared in 1935, and it used a specially developed overhead-valve cylinder head — this, on the 2½ litre engine, remained in production until 1951, in company with a 3½ litre version until it was superceeded by the famous XK engine. The engine compartment shown here belongs to Brian Lewis's 1949 3½ litre saloon.

A highlight of the three-day event for the club was the visit on Monday of Sir William and Lady Lyons, who spent some time at the stand taking a good look at the exhibits. Here they examine the engine compartment of Bill Athawes' E-type.

Conducting the founder of Jaguar Cars round the club stand was Tom Fulford, who with a small band of members spent the weekend manning the club caravan and stand — his own XJ coupe was on display too, and is seen in the foreground.

Also inspected was John Owen's lovely SS 100, which with the SS 90 was Jaguar's first sports car.

Sir William was highly impressed by Dan Kennedy's XK 150S roadster, which he thought that like Bill Athawes' E-type, was "better than it left us new"!

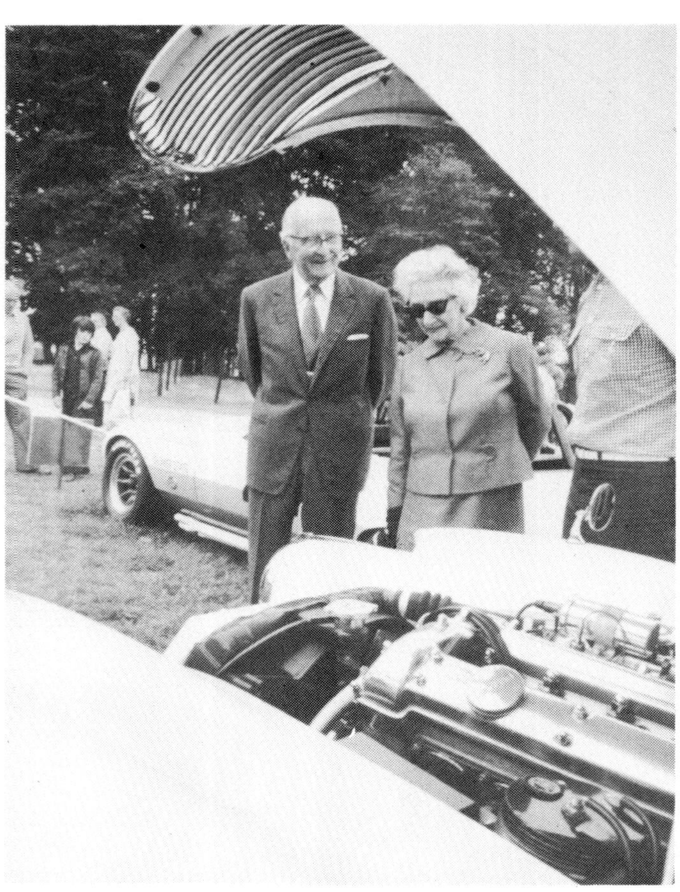

Sir William and Lady Lyons did not neglect to visit the club caravan, where the faithful bunch of helpers were dispensing club accessories, books and other paraphenalia. Lady Lyons even selected a JDC T-shirt for her grandson.

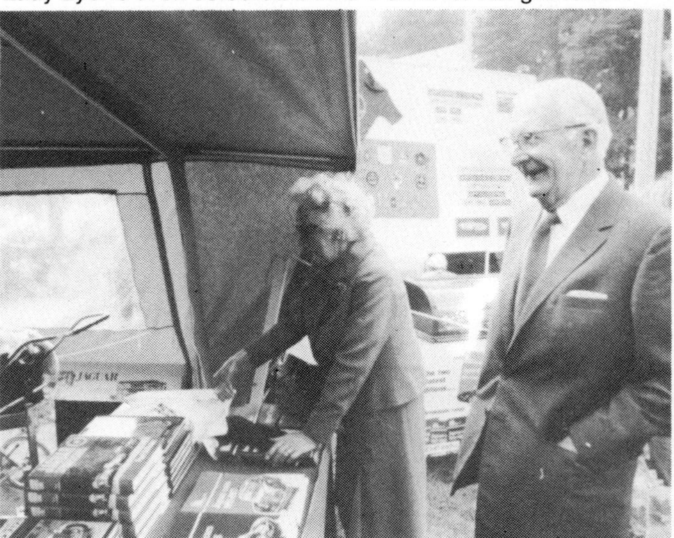

As Jaguar grew, so it absorbed other manufacturers — examples were included on the club stand, such as a Coventry Climax racing engine, and as shown here with Sir William, a Guy truck and a Daimler bus.

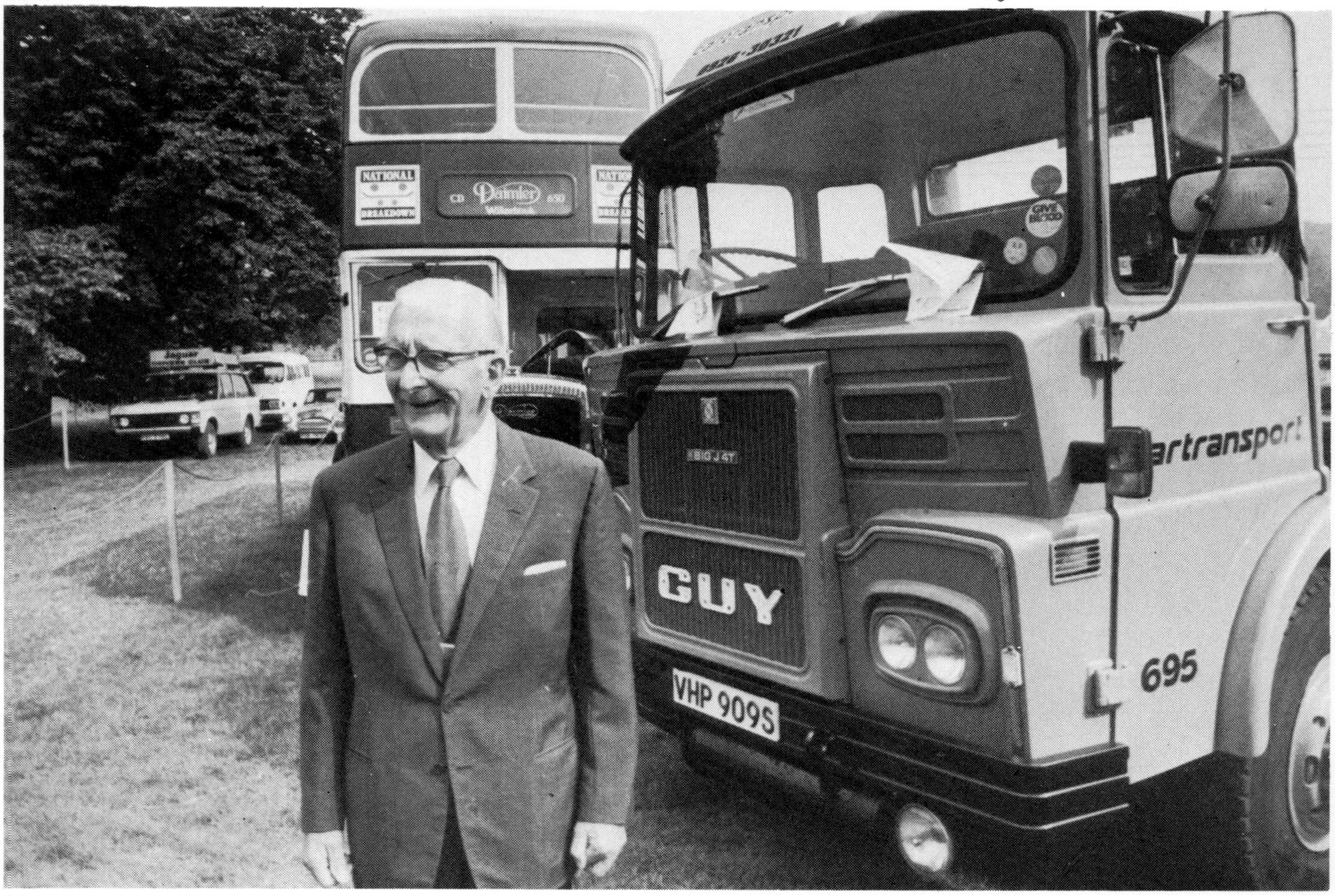

Bill Athawes' 4.2 E-type gained the premier 'Best British Car of the Show' award — see colour section too.

Then the 1971-1978 Open Road Car class was captured by Alan Hames' primrose yellow V12 E-type in another victory for 'our' marque.

Besides the club team cars, members could enter their Jaguars individually at Stoneliegh as this line-up shows — Wilfird Moss's XK 120 fixed-head is in the foreground, with the Mk VII saloon of Robert Pettit next.

Yet more — Gerry Margrave receiving his winnings after his 420 saloon had been placed first in the 1961-1970 Closed Road Car class.

Supporting the outright winners was Geoffrey Diffey's 2-plus-2 V12 E-type, its second place adding to the string of Jaguar successes at Stoneleigh; no other marque could approach Jaguar's domination of the concours classes.

Stars of the Show: Dan Kennedy's XK 150S open two seater, and John Owen's SS 100. Dan achieved a win in the 1945-1960 Open Road Cars class, while John was second in the PVT 1931-1948 class.

SOUTHERN JAGUAR DAY

Effingham Park, that impressive car and conference centre near Crawley, Surrey, was the scene of the first Southern Jaguar Day held by the club. It was organised by the Kent Area, and attracted a big turn-out. A small portion of the Jaguars present is shown in this Mike Beales picture.

Needless to say, there was a concours, and the judges are seen at work here, with Graham Bigg holding the clip-board. A line of Mk IIs are undergoing scrutiny at this point. *Photo Mike Beales.*

Big saloons at Effingham Park — XJs too can be spotted in this group of Mk IIs and 420G, and certainly current models are coming to club events in ever-increasing numbers. *Photo Mike Beales.*

The Kent Area had their own display at Effingham Park, with a spread of models embracing SS 100, XJ6, XK 150, and XJ coupe. *Photo: Mike Beales.*

YEOVIL FESTIVAL OF MOTORING

This neat SS2 came to Yeovil, virtually faultless in presentation and originality. *Photo: Stuart Sadd*

Rare survivor at Yeovil was this Swift Swallow, one of the original cars to be re-bodied by William Lyons' coachbuilding firm in Blackpool. *Photo: Stuart Sadd.*

This Somerset event is always well liked, and JDC members are to be seen there in considerable numbers. Here is a group of Jaguars on the display field. *Photo: Stuart Sadd.*

INTERNATIONAL XK DAY

XK Day is always a popular meeting, even though XKs themselves are becoming rarer, and are often outnumbered at their own events. The classic lines of an XK 150, with rows of XKs in the background.

Kevin Donnelly's ex-Alpine Rally car won the XK 120 concours class — in the opinion of the judges, "the best compromise of condition, originality and use".

Almost a foregone conclusion — Dan Kennedy's XK 150S roadster took home the Elite Class award for previous winners, and that for 'Best Overall XK'.

XK enthusiasts come from all over Europe to XK Day —
here's an XK 150 drophead coupe, basking in the sun which
this year's event (held on Sept 17th) was blessed with. Thirty
XK 150s came to Dodington Park, amongst them Roel
Zandee's award-winning coupe shown here. Rob Saunders
of the East Midlands Centre brought his XK 140 to XK Day,
and was one of only 12 XK 140 owners to do so.
Photo: John Williams

As always, there was the Club Caravan to man — or in this case, very definitely to woman. The helpers shown here are Lynne and Carolyn, obviously having a busy time dispensing club accessories, books and advice.

XK ancestor — the original XK 120 of 1948 used a shortened version of the Mk V saloon chassis, and at least one Mk V came to XK Day, in company with its 'Mk IV' predecessor, a handsome drophead in black.

Saloons too — Mk Is and IIs at Dodington, where as can be seen the park provided lots of space for the assembled Jaguars. Just off the M4 near Chipping Sodbury, the location was easy to get to for most people as well.

It seems as if only five Mk VII/VIII/IX cars came to XK Day, and at least two of these travelled from abroad — surely we're not eventually going to become outnumbered by our friends from the continent?

No less than 74 'E' types came to Dodington, outnumbering XKs
and every other individual type. Very much the coming car!

Winner of the XK 'Distance Award' went to Karl Heinz Bolling, who
drove his XK 140 drophead 650 miles to XK Day!

SS Jaguar 100, one of Britain's best-known sports cars whose fame far outstretches the numbers built by S.S. Cars Ltd – a mere 308 were completed between 1936 and 1940. The 3½ litre version was capable of just on 100mph.

Photo: Paul Skilleter

SCOTTISH JAGUAR DAY

The Scottish section of the JDC is growing rapidly, and Scottish Jaguar Day has become an important part of the club's calendar. A star attraction this year was undoubtedly Campbell McLaren's XKSS, finished in Ecurie Ecosse blue. *Photo: David Harvey.*

Campbell surveys his car, obviously pleased with his 'Best Car of Day' award. Numbers indicate the car's entry in the hill climb run at the same time, as Doune was the venue for Scottish Jaguar Day.
Photo: David Harvey.

A beautifully presented car — the flawless lines of Sandy Carnegie's 1956 XK 140 fixedhead. From Arbroath, the car was originally registered HHH 566; it must be one of the best north of the border.
Photo: David Harvey.

Three generations. . . Interested onlookers with Stephen Allen's
1948 2½ litre saloon, which was recently on display in the Glasgow
Transport Museum.   *Photo: David Harvey.*

Gathering of the clans? Or international trade federation
conference? David Cottingham (left) with Bob and Betty Kerr, and
John Harper who had a go up Doune's narrow, sleeper-lined hill with
Bob's 'E' type.   *Photo: David Harvey.*

Undoubtedley the supreme XK 150 of 1978 was Dan Kennedy's 'S' open two seater. Dan comes from the United States, and decided to bring his car with him during a tour of duty in England. Restored to the highest standards, the XK 150 was presented with the 'Best XK' award at International XK Day in 1978 — one of many accolades the car has received while it has been in this country.

They've some good registration numbers in Scotland! The 'E' type belongs to the XK 150 is the late Jock Campbell's which is now brought to JDC events by Malcolm Frisby, while 'BK' is Bob Kerr's ex-Burbidge racing 'E' type which is now doing so well in Scottish events.

David Cunningham, a very active Scottish JDC member, with an M registered XK 150, and a Mk V saloon as background. *Photo: David Harvey.*

Some nice Mk IIs at Doune. . . .

. . .matched by some equally pleasant XK 150s. *Photos: David Harvey.*

MK1 / MK11 DAY

XKs at Mk II Day — but as always, everyone comes to each Register day regardless of the type being celebrated. Most of these XKs seem to be fitted with 15-inch wheels, incidentally — originally, the rim size was 16-inch, but it's easier to get radial tyres for the smaller diameter. *Photo: Mike Beales.*

Old-timer line-up: 'Mk IV' Jaguar saloons with a very rare, early-style SS2. These big saloons were incidentally never officially known as Mk IV by the factory, but were inevitably so described when replaced by the Mk V of 1948/49. *Photo: Mike Beales.*

NATIONAL CLASSIC & COLLECTORS CAR SHOW

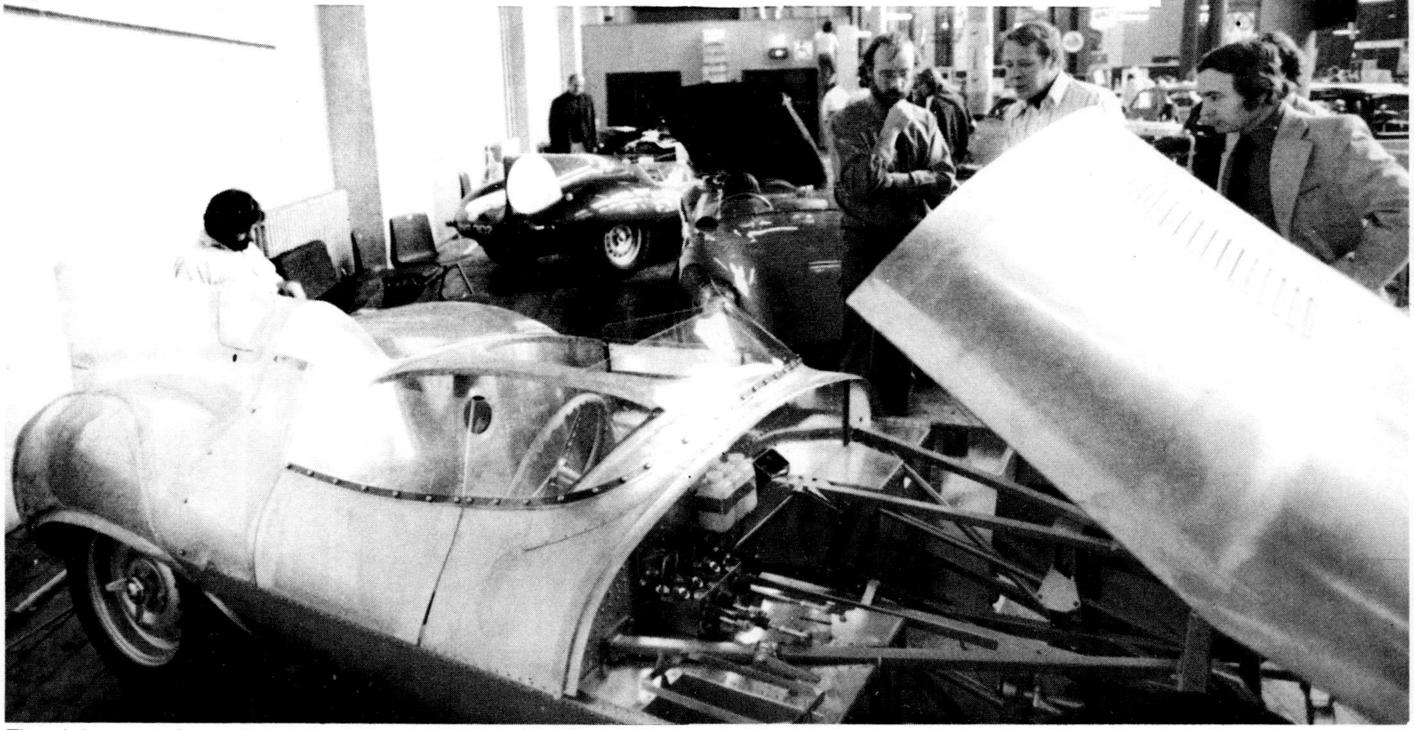

The club manned a well-organised stand at this year's Classic Car Show at the Alexandra Palace, which also contained other exhibits of interest to Jaguar enthusiasts — such as the superb D-type replicas made by the Lynx Motor Company (foreground, minus engine), and their historic car restorations which included MWS 302, the ex-Ecurie Ecosse 'real' D-type. *Photo: Stuart Sadd.*

Also on show at Alexandra Palace was this very straight, original XK 140 fixed-head coupe, which formed part of Rod Leach's 'Nostalgia' stand.

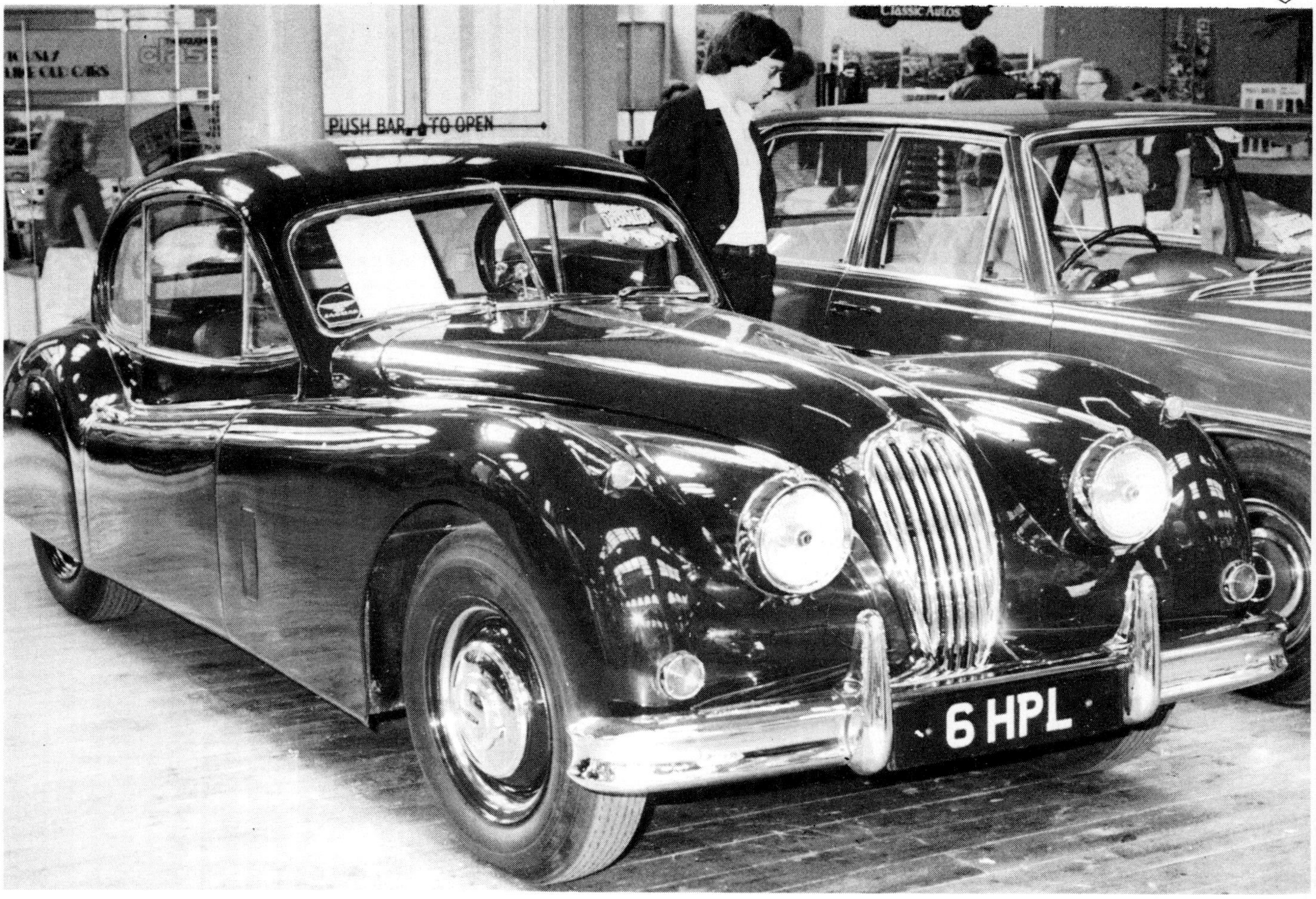

THE MOTOR SHOW BIRMINGHAM

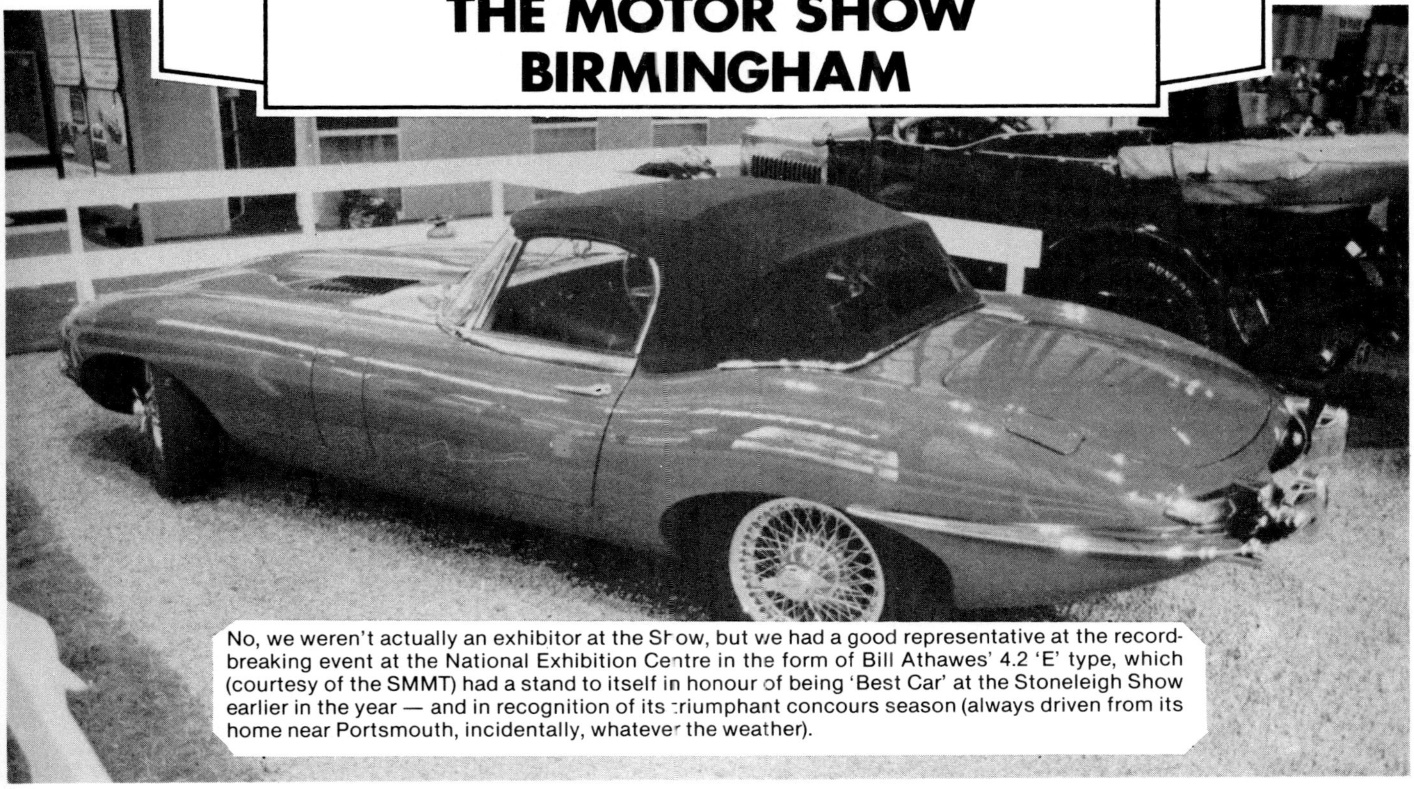

No, we weren't actually an exhibitor at the Show, but we had a good representative at the record-breaking event at the National Exhibition Centre in the form of Bill Athawes' 4.2 'E' type, which (courtesy of the SMMT) had a stand to itself in honour of being 'Best Car' at the Stoneleigh Show earlier in the year — and in recognition of its triumphant concours season (always driven from its home near Portsmouth, incidentally, whatever the weather).

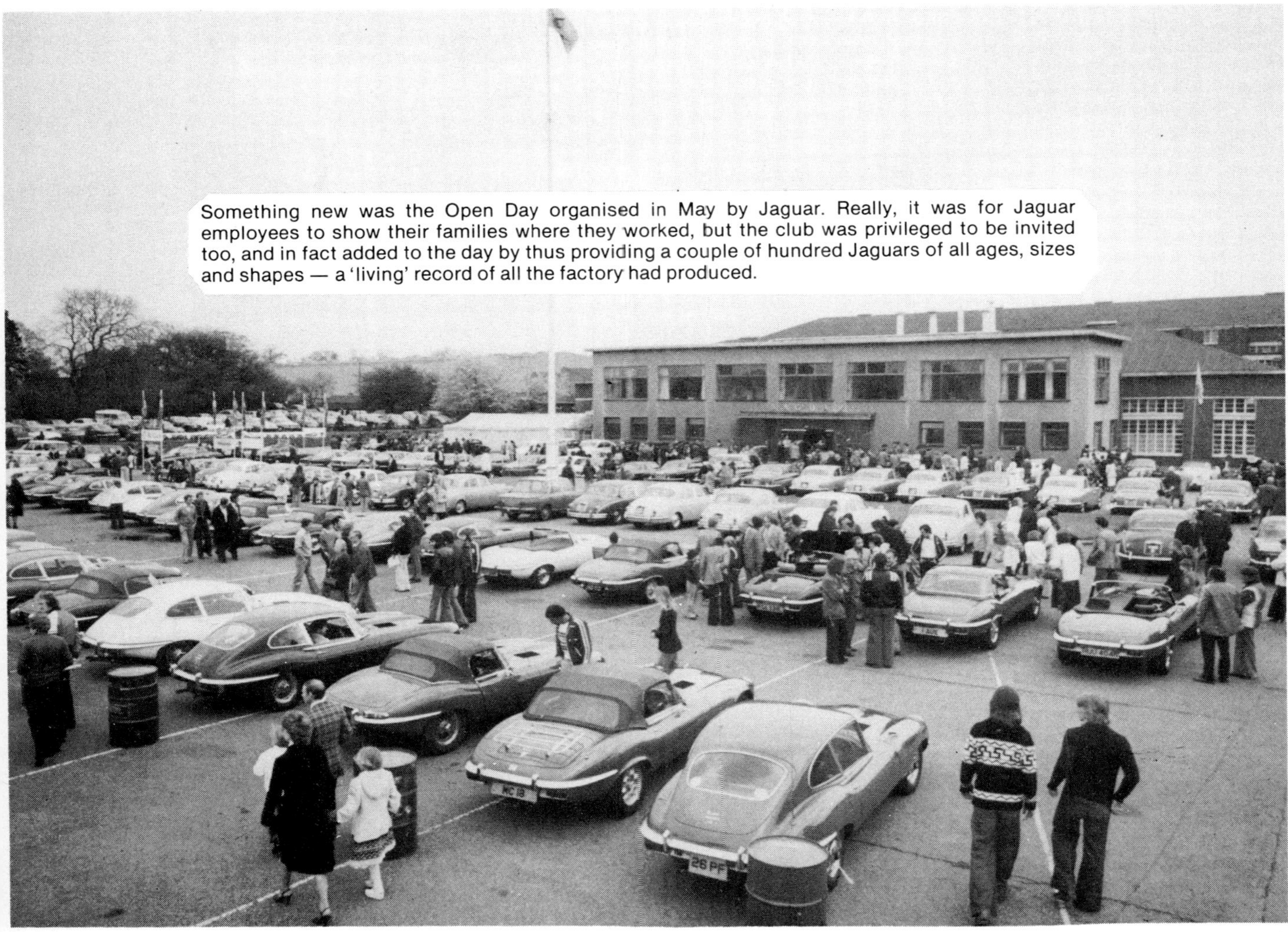

Something new was the Open Day organised in May by Jaguar. Really, it was for Jaguar employees to show their families where they worked, but the club was privileged to be invited too, and in fact added to the day by thus providing a couple of hundred Jaguars of all ages, sizes and shapes — a 'living' record of all the factory had produced.

ANNUAL GENERAL MEETING

Every year, the club meets at Jaguar's factory at Browns Lane, Allesley, Coventry for the Annual General Meeting. Every year it rains. However, this does little to damp the spirits of those assembling, revived by tea and cakes laid on by Jaguar, and enjoying a good look round the famous entrance hall with its superb exhibits. An S.S.2. radiator braves the elements outside.

XKs in a reflective mood? And these were the sort of conditions which the concours judges had to cope with, because the AGM sees the awarding of the HR Owen 'Champion of Champions. trophy.

Not as bad as it seems! It may appear that this 420 has met a sticky end after a desperate piece of high speed driving, but in fact it all happened at about 3mph, during precise manoueverings in the 'inter-Centre' driving tests at Browns Lane.

One of the tests involved keeping all four wheels astride a tortuously traced white line marked on the car park. Particularly difficult, perhaps, with the biggest of all Jaguars, the 420G saloon. The tests were won by the organising centre, Kent, but they'd dearly love great participation — and competition — at next year's event.

420G, XK 140 and 'E' type at Browns Lane for the AGM.

Mks VII and VIII outside the entrance hall at Jaguar, bonnets open for the concours judges. The Champion of Champions' trophy though eventually went to Gerry Margrave's 420 saloon in a very close finish.

Rare Jaguar — this is a 1936 SS Jaguar Tourer, one of very few which were built during the run of the first 'Jaguar' range made by SS Cars from 1935 to 1937. There was no drophead coupe version of the new Jaguar saloon range which replaced the S.S.1 in 1935, so a version of the S.S.1 tourer body was mounted on the new chassis. It was dropped at the end of 1937, when the all-steel range of Jaguars came into being, replaced by a conventional drophead version of the saloon. This superb example is owned by David Middleton of Wolverhampton, who restored it from a complete wreck purchased in 1967 for £10! *Photo: Paul Skilleter*

Twin Test

*Paul Skilleter drove two very different
Jaguars round Mallory at E-Type Day,
and here's what he found.*

John Pearson at speed in the ex-Jack Lambert roadster; Dunlop alloy wheels are
fitted, of modest rim width and within the bodywork.

John Pearson is a very generous fellow and seems to
spend most of his time lending cars to people — it's
his Lister-Jaguar which Michael Bowler of 'Thoroughbred & Classic Cars' has been charging round in so
successfully this season, and neither did he bat an
eyelid when I hinted at E-Type Day in June that I
wouldn't mind a drive in his 'historic' E-type, not
having brought anything myself to take advantage of
the track test facilities on offer that day.

I already knew the car quite well; it started off life in
1961 as RL 26, driven successfully in club and national
races by its first owner Jack Lambert; a shunt
prompted the fitting of aluminium bonnet, doors and
bootlid, plus larger brakes and big-valve, Webered
engine. Then tragedy struck, as a mechanic took the
car for an unauthorised drive on the road, crashed
fatally and almost wrote it off. It was rebuilt by John
Harper to Group 3 trim, with SU carburettors and
standard valves and cams, and raced jointly with Mick
Merrick in several long-distance GT events in 1966,
finishing 2nd in class at Spa, and again at the
Nurburgring 1000km behind a works 275GTB Ferrari.

It was John Harper who repurchased the car many
years later, and rebuilt it back to early-sixties racing
specification. Since acquiring the car himself, John

Pearson has done a lot more sorting, and has been a
competitive and consistent entrant with it over the
past couple of seasons, despite its engine
specification being way behind most of the other
Jaguars competing in Group 2 Historic racing.

Getting into the car, I was at once very much at ease
in the comfortable leather bucket seat, behind the big,
familiar old E-type wood-rimmed wheel John has kept.
The engine started instantly, and ticked over calmly.
After a bit of a wait to get out on the circuit, we were off
— and my first impression was how good the gear-
change was. It is, in fact, rather a special 3.8 box,
having synchromesh on all four gears, work carried out
by the factory some time back in the car's past.

The second impression was, what an easy car to
drive! The only problem concerned getting into the
groove again after a couple of years off the track,
especially as I'd not driven round Mallory before.
Fortunately, Graig Hinton came to the rescue —
looming in the rear view mirror came a towering, dark
green monster, not Graig himself but Graig in his
classic racing Mk VII Jaguar saloon, at all sorts of
angles and obviously determined to get by.

Of course, the E-type was far quicker that the Mk VII
but we circulated side by side for a couple of laps until

I remembered you're supposed to drive fast in a racing car on a circuit. It just needed that spur to get me driving a little more aggresively, and a grinning Graig Hinton provided it. Once free from the clutches of the big saloon, it was easy to draw away and to begin considering the very real qualities of the E-type.

Without doubt, it was the best mannered, best handling E-type I'd ever driven on a track; it was so smooth and predictable as to be ridiculously easy to drive, and you'd really have to be stupid to get in any sort of trouble. The brakes were powerful and progressive, and the whole car felt amazingly well balanced through the corners, with the back end almost correcting itself as you powered away from a bend.

It certainly wasn't the fastest E-type I'd driven, that honour probably belonging to the JCB lightweight E-type that Willie Green used to drive, but it was by far and away the most pleasant, and much more progressive than the JCB car. Everything in the suspension and steering felt like it was working correctly, and with that ultra smooth engine pulling away in front, the whole car felt as if it would be capable of finishing a Le Mans race the next weekend.

When I pulled in, I was amazed to hear John say that I'd been out there for half-an-hour — I could hardly believe it, as to me it had felt more like ten minutes! I don't think I've ever enjoyed 30 minutes on a circuit so much before, and I climbed out of the red E-type feeling that this really was 'my' sort of car.

Much of the 'professional' feel of this car — which in John's hands was quicker than all but one of the wide-wheeled mod-sports E-types at Mallory that day

POS pulls in after an enjoyable half-hour round Mallory. A bearded Graig Hinton seems amused, while John is only too grateful to don his helmet for another go himself!

Attention to detail is exemplified by aluminium panelled boot. A larger fuel tank takes up the space normally occupied by the spare wheel. ▽

Pilot's seat in the 'E' type. Note the standard steering wheel, considered the best for quick response, a larger tachometer reading to 8,000 rpm (though rarely is more than 6,000 rpm actually used), and the in-car fire extinguishing tubing on the transmission tunnel. ▽

Our cover cars — the classic shape of E-type roadster, and the 420 Jaguar saloon, one of the last 'compact' Jaguars to come from Coventry. They are shown together just after they had won their respective classes at the National Classic Car Concours at Weston Park, Shropshire in July. Bill Athawes' 1965 4.2 E-type took away the 'Best Car of Show' award too, and later in the year was displayed at the Motor Show, Birmingham. Gerry Margrave's 1968 automatic 420 rounded off its concours season by being elected 'Champion of Champions' at the Club's AGM concours in October.
Photo: Paul Skilleter

John Pearson (centre) discusses his 'E' type with a mod-sport 'E' driver. Vents in bootlid a la lightweight 'E' allow hot air to escape from the rear brakes. Petrol filler protruding through lid allows fuel to be added without having to raise the lid. Roll-over bar is situated under the 'works' glass fibre hard-top.

— is due to the person who prepares it with John, and that's Bill Nicholson. Many will associate Bill with the ultra-rapid MGB which he's campaigned for many years now, but for a long time he was a development engineer at Jaguar. That his work included the factory's lightweight E-type programme in 1963/64 goes a long way to explaining exactly why this E-type feels the true thoroughbred it is.

Bill in fact wants to develop the car further, though I feel John himself half wants to keep it as it is — ''you just get in and drive it, take it home again, and put it in the garage until the next race'', he says. But whatever thay eventually decide to do, I'm sure that the 1979 season will see the red roadster lapping Silverstone as immaculately as ever, an object lesson in E-type preparation.

I say, James, the back end's going

That immortal phrase was coined when 'Motor' tested a gigantic presidential-type Lincoln limousine. A Mk VII may be smaller but after that E-type, it didn't feel it.

With no disrespect to Graig Hinton's steed at all, the E-type was about the worst possible car I could have driven immediately before stepping up into the Mk VII saloon. Its swervability and precision steering made it seem as if one was swopping from a Derby winner to a bull elephant with toothache — both quite fast in a straight line but with vastly different characteristics on reaching the corner at the end.

MK VII (yes, that's its real registration!) left Browns Lane in 1952, and went to an old lady who was always chauffeur-driven. The car's original registration was SVK 140, and it eventually passed to the chauffeur — from whom Graig bought the car in 1973, for the then handsome sum of £345. Graig had bought a 120 with MKV 11 on it, and had been looking for the best Mk VII he could find to hang the number on.

Then came Classic Saloon Racing, from which the motor sporting world has never totally recovered. They said it would be ludicrous, just a huge joke, and it would never work. They were right — about the first two things; but almost at once the Championship for pre-1957 (loosely) cars also proved itself to be a competitive, exciting and very enjoyable branch of the sport, and it's gone from strength to strength ever since. Graig has always been in the thick of it, running the Mk VII and TVC 254, his 2.4 Mk I, with the larger car now the veteran of over 50 races and two Champion-ship class wins — some record!

Now I've actually raced TVC a couple of times, but had always managed to avoid being put in the driving seat of the Mk VII, despite various attempts at getting me there. However, my excuses ran out at Mallory, so there I was, plonked behind the big steering wheel and peering loftily over the rooftops of other cars; in the distance, at the end of the bonnet, I could catch a glimpse of the track. Graig helped me fasten the harness, and I heard the 'snick' of the padlock as he withdrew from the cockpit; it was too late — I was trapped.

So on with the ignition and press the starter button on the wooden dash panel. An instant response from the engine, so no let-out there. Despite its Isky cams, the 3.4 engine idled well, though a touch of the throttle brought instant stimulation to the rev counter, thanks to the lightened flywheel. It wasn't even very noisy, as much of the interior trim remained, and the two 2-inch SU carbs didn't make the sucking noise typical of a row of Webers.

Into gear, clutch up gently, and we moved off — seemingly ponderous at first, then as the revs picked up, surging forward impressively and very smoothly. Yes, that was definitely a corner looming up, and we were in third gear and probably well on the way to 90 mph. Right, so we'll give the brakes a dab — yes, nicely servoed and with a good response — then we'll give the wheel a turn and round we'll go.

But hang on — what's this? Surely the wheel's been round once, but we're still heading for the outside bank. Directional stability is all very well, but . . . Let's try another turn — ah yes, we feel a distinct movement at the front — not much mind you, but an encourage-ment to give another pull. And then, rather like a supertanker coming into dock (if supertankers do go into docks), we swing into the bend with a distinct roll and a token protest from the radial tyres.

Having accomplished a change of direction, we continue on the same lock round the long right-hander, and still in third gear, experiment with some throttle. Almost at once it's time to change up, and with top gear engaged, we steam round the back of Mallory, getting faster and faster. Then there's that funny right-hander and the wiggle-woggle through the esses (it's the short circuit) and back onto the pits straight again — which causes a lurch or two and some rapid wheel twiddling to keep pointing vaguely in the right direction.

This time we're ready for the bends at the end of the straight, and get a good 1½ turns on the wheel sometime before the corner actually comes up. The technique seems to work, and with another turn for good measure as we come into the bend, we take up what is bordering on an oversteering attitude which is held on the throttle. You hardly need to have changed down to third, such is the torque from the engine, and once more top gear is selected for the long right-hand bend which merges into the shortish back straight on the other side of Mallory's lake.

A few more laps confirm one's early impressions. Graig is mad to race this car at the speeds at which he does. Then a couple more laps, and we feel that, maybe, he's not mad but just a trifle eccentric. After all, the Mk IX discs with their Mk II servo assistance do appear to work very well, and once the steering's voracious appetite for armfuls of lock is satiated by the required amount of arm twirling, the car does indeed begin to handle very predictably.

Mind you, like all elephants, you have to show it who's master. It's no good nosing into a corner under braking, caressing the wheel and applying the throttle to carry it through from mild understeer to equally mild oversteer, like with the E-type. No, you have to dictate what is to happen, and you certainly can't afford to

The Beast — Graig and the Mk VII at Silverstone, in an unusually controlled-looking pose.

Yes, he does this *every* lap . . .

allow it to choose for itself when it's going to oversteer, because even should your arms disappear into a blur as they wind on opposite lock, it would be far too late to catch it. Much better to get all the winding done first, so that the back begins to come round at the start of the corner, by which time you've already begun the counter-attack by twirling in the opposite direction.

Mind you, I hardly emulated the regular pilot's prowess in this respect as it required considerably more nerve than I possessed, and I have this odd urge to keep living — quaint. However, even Graig met his match with the car later on in the season, and very sad to relate crunched it rather heavily at Donington in October.

Fortunately, apart from some bruises, all was OK and in fact he went racing the next day at Brands, using Mick Sherwin's very standard Mk VIII saloon; this was interesting, because Mick had once let me drive this car at a practice session at Silverstone, and after trying Graig's car, I felt that the Mk VIII as I remembered it handled and steered better. Having put the bog-standard engined VIII on the front row of the grid at Brands, Graig confirmed my opinion in this matter — it's peculiar how two similar cars can behave so differently for no apparant reason, because there were no chassis changes introduced when the Mk VIII superceeded the Mk VII in 1956.

This episode at Mallory certainly reminded me what fun classic saloon racing is, and how much people like Graig have added to it, with their unfailing appearances and unquenchable enthusiasm. As for the old lady herself, it looks as if at last, this final brush with the Armco has broken even her stout old back, and when MKV 11 appears again next season, it may be on a new chassis. But appear again it will, you can depend upon it!

□ □ □

STOP THE ROT

An in-depth guide to protecting the E-type Jaguar from rust.
By Paul Skilleter.

Ready for work — the writer's 1962 fixed-head E-type undergoing its annual treatment which has helped it retain all its original panels.

If you own an E-type, you'll know that the biggest problem in running it is keeping the bodywork in one piece. Like any car of its period, the construction of the E-type is inclined to encourage attack from rust, and about four or five years is the maximum one can expect before holes appear — in fact, it can happen in less time even than that, and neither is a particularly heavy mileage required.

However, there's a lot you can do to keep the dreaded enemy at bay, so long as serious corrosion is not already well established — it's no good attempting preventative measures on a car which really needs a cure; the only way to combat actual rot is to cut out the affected area and let-in new panels. So the following is aimed at the owner with a car which is either generally well preserved, or has already been repaired as necessary.

We'll begin at the front, with the bonnet. If there are any signs of bubbling under the paint along the beading which separates the two wings from the big centre section, or you can poke holes in the bulkhead behind the headlights, forget it — your best bet is probably to buy a new bonnet from Jaguar, which considering it accounts for one-third of the length of the car, is good value at around £400. But assuming it's sound, the work begins with a good clean of the underside.

You can employ a steam cleaner, but that won't relieve you of a lot of necessary hand-work so resign yourself to getting dirty! A good soaking with a garden hose will help shift the mud, then close in on the danger spots with an old stiff paintbrush or blunt chisel to remove built-up deposits of road dirt from every corner of the bulkhead in front of the wheels (especially around the hinge mountings, and in the corners where bulkhead meets wing), and from either side of the wing/bonnet flanges. Get as much dirt as you can out of the flange 'sandwich', and if you're careful, you may be able to bend the tabs of the chrome beading piece and gently remove it in order to clean between wing and bonnet centre even more thoroughly; this means you'll also need to undo the bonnet/wing nuts, distance washers and bolts too, and in the case of Series II and III cars, the chrome headlamp finisher — though be careful not to break off the clips.

Other points to clean are the corners of the bulkhead behind the front wheels, and along the wired edge of the wing itself. It really is essential to be very thorough, because whatever you coat the underside with afterwards isn't going to stick to mud. Having made sure all's clean, tackle any surface rust both by grinding it off wherever possible, or neutralising it with products such as Trustan, Nuetra-Rust, Naval Jelly and so on. I also use Bondaprimer on sound metal surfaces where the original sealant has come adrift and left the metal exposed.

You now need to cover all these danger areas with something which will protect them in the future. I favour Tectyl for this job, which comes in a two-aerosol pack — underbody and internal (ML) grades. The pack costs less than £3.00, and as you rarely need to coat the flat under-parts of a car, two or three packs will probably suffice for an E-type. Spray the underbody material along all joins and into all corners, continuing with a paintbrush if necessary, and make sure you get as much as possible between the flanges (before replacing the beading if that's been removed).

You're not finished with the bonnet yet though — there's the hollow nose sections to be taken care of now. Access to these are best gained through the sidelight apertures — remove the units by unscrewing and don't bother to disconnect the wiring as there's enough slack to allow them to hang clear of the hole. A torch will reveal the state of the metal inside, and try to remove any flaking rust especially along the ledge which you'll see. Use a long screwdriver or stiff bottle brush, and push the debris out of the drain hole at the bottom of the cavity.

About the best medium for protecting such as the bonnet internals is Waxoyl, which I've used for some years with success. It's based on paraffin wax and contains various anti-rust agents including calcium sulphanate and amines; it's unique amongst rust preventing fluids in that its makers claim it kills existing rust besides merely protecting good metal, and my experiences back this up. Waxoyl can be applied by Finnigan's own syringe, or by one of those hand-trigger squirters you buy in gardening shops. Anyway, ladle the stuff in generously, and attempt to cover every part of the bonnet internals, including where the bumper bolts protrude inside.

In the case of earlier E-types with the closed headlights, it's as well to remove the Triplex glass covers and treat around the headlights, and wherever else you can reach. On all cars, check the headlight 'scoop' in front of the light unit, and ensure that drain holes are clear.

A further cavity is contained in the lower nose under the air intake, and this too should be liberally sprayed. Usually, there are drain holes through which you can do this, and some cars have a removable rubber bung

which is where overseas licence plates would be fitted.

Final measures on the bonnet should include spraying Waxoyl or Tectyl down the air intake and heater ducts, along all internal seams, and into the box section 'hoop' round the circumference of the bonnet at the car's bulkhead end. It's quite possible to preserve a 'concours' appearance on the underside of the bonnet despite these measures, as having allowed time for the material to creep right into all the seams, you can wipe off the surplus with a white-spirit soaked rag, and finish with a good wax polish. Lastly, on the outside of the bonnet, it's a good idea to run fluid down the wing beading, and all round chrome fixtures and under the bumpers — again removing the excess before polishing off.

Next section to tackle is the car's front bulkhead. This is a hollow horseshoe, the ends of which meet the sill on either side. The internal construction is not simple however, due to the presence of various internal panels (see pictures). There are two main access points — the outer skin of the bulkhead where it meets the sill can be protected through the holes found underneath the bonnet clamps, on the front face of the bulkhead under the bonnet; remove the rubber bung and squirt your material in, at various angles. Don't forget to replace the bung.

The remainder of the bulkhead has to be tackled from the inside of the car. It is possible to insert a probe through the hinge points on the door shut face, but better still, remove the bonnet release handles by unscrewing them (noting the number of turns so you can replace them correctly), and unscrew the escutcheon plate. Then peel back the vinyl trim, to reveal a large vertical hole on the inside face of the bulkhead (on later cars, you may also have to detach the fresh-air vent control).

Working through this, you should be able to reach all the major parts of the structure, using a probe (see notes on applicators at end). You should even be able to run a tube up into the 'dog-leg' windscreen pillar support, which is a dangerous rust point on an E-type.

The same access point can be the start of the sill protection procedure, because there's a horizontal hole leading straight into the main sill; sometimes it's covered by a rubber diaphragm. Insert your probe here, and be generous with the material; refer to the pictures, and wriggle the probe about so you also get inside the flitch-plate which bisects the diameter of

The outer sills are the most obvious places for rust to show, and can often reach the stage where they can be torn away from the car by hand. This indicates the almost certain existence of rot in the inner sill too. The door on this car has also decayed badly. ▽

The sill on this car has been roughly cut away, but very apparent is the rot in another common place, the closed section in the side wall of the front bulkhead. This area can be treated via the rubber-bunged hole in the front face of the bulkhead. ▽

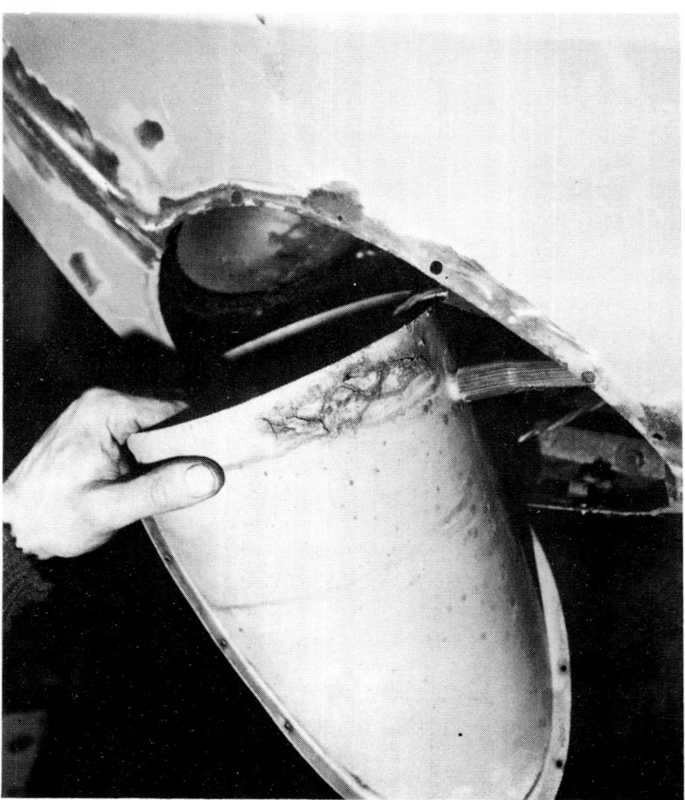

Regular inspection of the headlight area is well advised. This picture shows how water has rotted out the bottom of the headlight 'scoop', probably because the drain hole or tube attached has become blocked.

Corrosion of the bonnet centre/wing flanges is usually fatal to the bonnet, and can rapidly lead to holes like this. Regular cleaning and protection is the only answer.

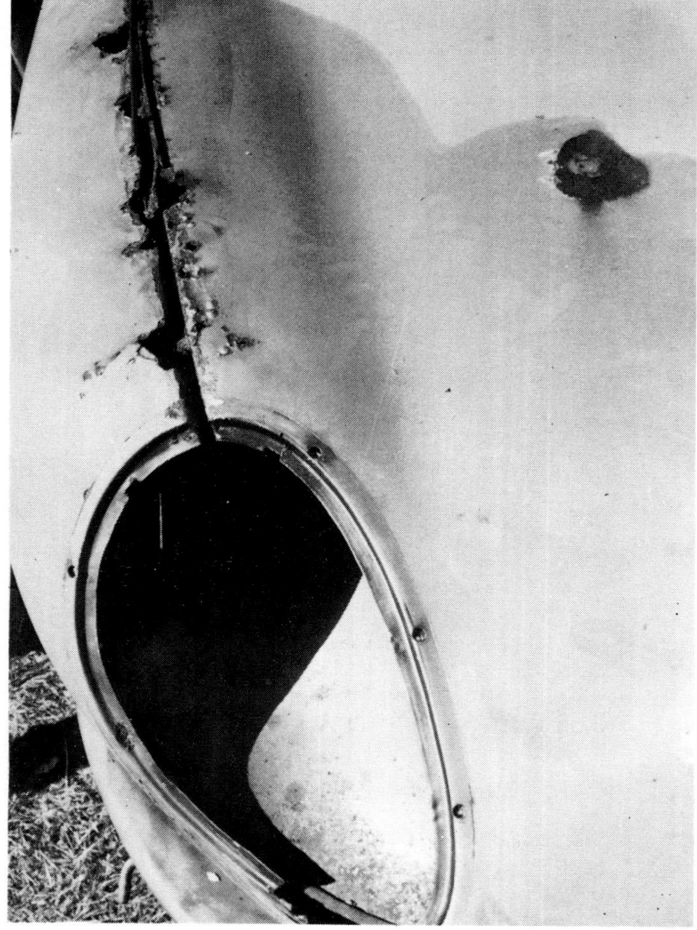

the sill at the point below the bulkhead.

If you wish to be properly thorough, remove the seats at this stage. This will allow you to locate the nylon-plugged holes on the inner face of the sill, at nearly floor level, though it will mean pulling up the vinyl covering a little way (easily stuck back). To be extra sure, you can also drill further holes on the inner face of the sill, using the channel in which the wiring loom runs (though obviously make sure the wires stay away from the drill bit!). The cross-member running across the car under the seats can also be drilled and injected, and while you're in the area, take out all the mats and carefully examine the floor seams, especially in the footwell. Rub down, nuetralise and paint any suspect areas, and also track down and plug any leaks, because the floor pan will otherwise soon rot out. I also impregnated the sound-deadening pad on the floor of my early 'E' with Tectyl, to stop it acting like a sponge.

On 2-plus-2 and Series III cars, you can also get into the sills via the quite generous drain holes, but for further work on early E-types, some drilling is involved. This is done on the closing plate in front of the rear wheel, and the aim is to get fluid both sides of the flitchplate which bisects the sill here; refer to the picture. On roadster models only, you can also drill higher up, to protect the boxed part of the outer skin, behind the door-shut plate. Always seal any holes drilled with rubber grommets or plastic plugs.

Running between the sills behind the seats on the E-type is a low bulkhead which is the provider of lateral stiffness for the rear part of the car. Unfortunately, it is composed of three separate compartments on each side and these are very prone to rotting out, especially the one which serves as the mounting point for the rear suspension radius arm.

This box can be treated by removing the vinyl or Hardura covering in the small luggage well behind the seats (in the fixed-head) and drilling a hole on the top face about ½-inch in from the flange, and 5½ inches from the outer end of the bulkhead, where it meets door shut face wall. Fluid entering here should prevent that all-important section from rotting out. The anchorage plate for the radius arm also bolts into the floor beyond the bulkhead under the seat, and should be inspected for rust there.

2-plus-2 cars and Series III E-types have a different rear bulkhead, much lower and filled with sound deadening fibre. Fortunately the construction is more open, and you can pull out the fibre (there's yards of it!), treat the cavities, and replace it. As the fibre readily soaks up and retains moisture, this is a very necessary exercise.

Now we come to the treatment of the rear side-quarters of the car. On fixed-head E-types, unclip the trim panel under the side window, also unscrewing the cubby-hole on early cars. You can now reach the vunerable outer/inner wing join above the wheelarch, and much of the boxed area aft of the door shut pillar — though this last is made up of several sections, in that there's an internal wall which runs down inside to join the sill, more or less in parallel with the outer skin; however, there are a few holes through which you should be able to insert your probe.

You will be able to push the probe a considerable way back, between inner and outer rear wings, from below the side window, and further access is available if you unclip the trim panel to the rear of the side window, over the luggage area. On the roadster, the

The hinge mounting area of the bonnet, and the crevices formed by
bulkhead and wing, are candidates for regular cleaning.

Access to the lower bonnet area is best obtained through removing
the sidelight unit, as is being demonstrated on this Series III V12 car.

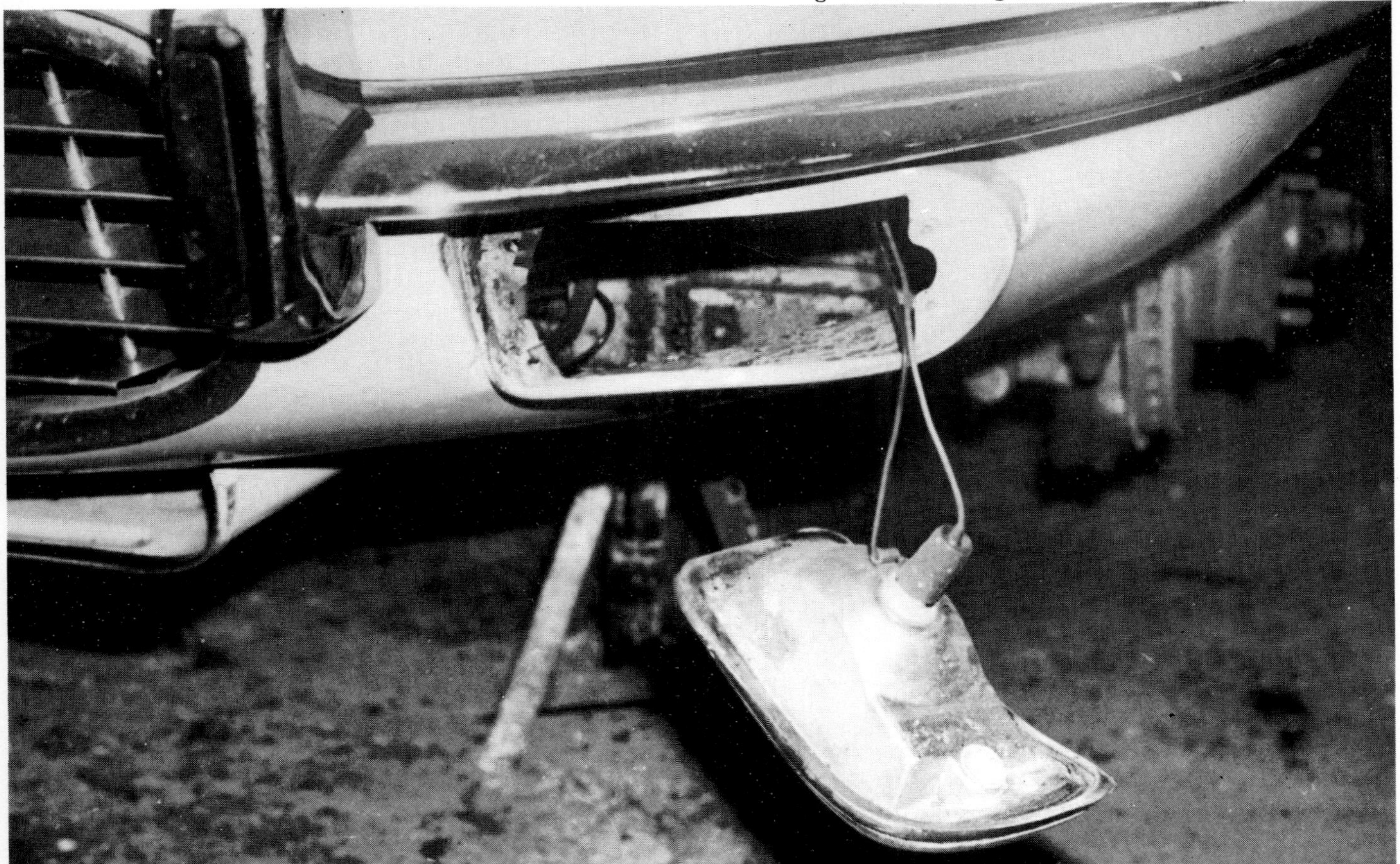

rear quarters can be reached by detaching the side panels in the boot, through which a surprising area can be covered.

Roadster models are a little different at the rear, as for a start they don't have a complete inner wing section — the outer wing is a single thickness above the rear wheel. As mentioned before, this allows you to protect the space between outer and inner skins behind the door shut face, by drilling a hole in the vertical panel in front of the wheel, about ¾-inch in from the outer edge, and 2½ inches up from the top of the sill, which is marked by a ledge.

On all models, it's essential to give the rear wheel arch a very good clean, paying special attention to ledges and seams, and to the 'lip' which surrounds the wheel arch. If no rust is present, protect with the under body material, coating the lips and ledges thickly. Some owners, incidentally, prefer to use a mastic sealant such as Evomastic to fill odd crevices and to round-off wing lips and wired edges so that water doesn't collect there. Personally, I prefer to rely on periodic inspection and touching-up with a thinner material, as I can never entirely persuade myself that something nasty isn't happening under a thick coating of sealant . . .

The sills of an E-type extend past the front bulkhead to carry the air cleaner on one side, and the battery on the other. It's a wise precaution to remove the battery and its tray at least once a year, swill out the entire area with fresh water, and then spray liberally with Waxoyl — battery acid is death to coachwork. At the same time, inspect the lower frame mounting point, where it bolts to the bulkhead; this is a danger spot on E-types, and it pays to regularly clean and inspect it, coating as necessary with Waxoyl or Tectyl.

On the other side of the car, get a good quantity of Waxoyl down below the air cleaner tub, and detach the undertray and clean off and treat the vacuum reservoir tank, which is often forgotten. This also provides an opportunity to spray something in the direction of the frame mounting on that side too.

Returning to the rear of the E-type, one closed section which must be protected is the panel which goes over the number plate recess. This can be tackled from inside, drilling the backing plate if necessary. Squirt material all the way along the rear of the car too, from the inside. Next, having removed the spare wheel and brushed out all loose dirt from the spare wheel well, allow Waxoyl to run down the longitudinal strengthening members. The well also has nylon-plugged holes at its lowest point, and I took most of mine out so that any water which got in could immediately run out again. All seams and joins should be cleaned out and treated with neutraliser, then painted, if surface rust has started. Make sure the drain hole in the spare wheel holder is clear, and treat that area too.

The kidney-shaped petrol tank can hide a great deal of damage, and really keen owners will remove it for a good look underneath. But a good measure of protection can also be obtained by injecting quantities of Waxoyl all round it — the probe can be pushed right around the back. With luck, the material should soak into the felt pads on which the tank rests, and into the foam plastic pad under the tank's sump/drain plug.

Outside, the under-panel at the rear of the E-type doesn't contain any particular rust traps (corrosion usually works its way from inside), but should be kept clean so that any rust spots will be noticed at once.

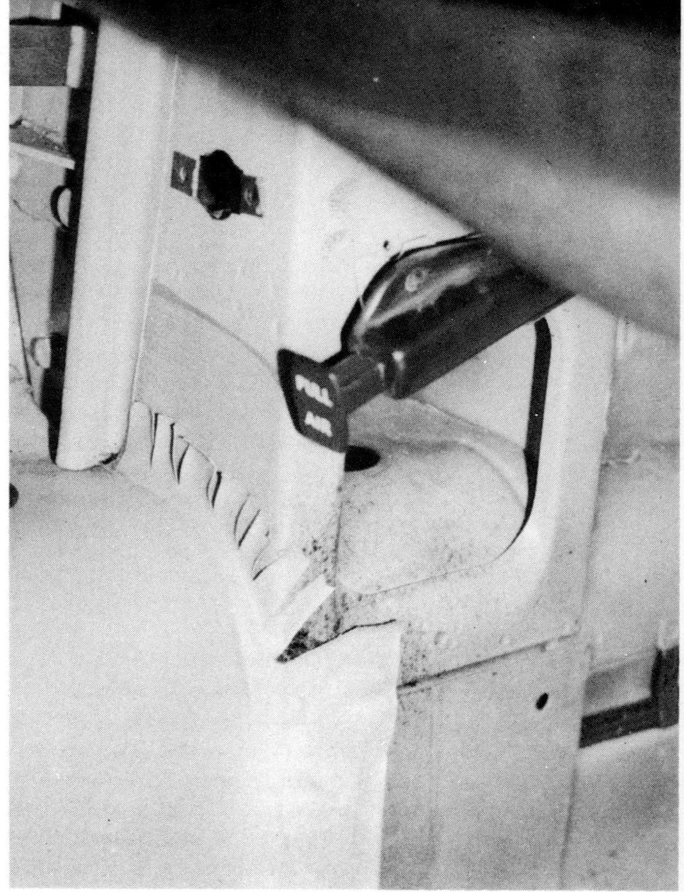

Front bulkhead and a good measure of main sill protection is achieved by reaching closed sections via this aperture, which is revealed by removing the side trim panel above the footwell; this requires the unscrewing of bonnet catch and (in later cars as shown on this Series III) the fresh-air vent lever. The hole down into the sill itself is visible, and a flexible probe will enable most of the 'horseshoe' bulkhead to be treated as well.

Even the side windscreen pillar support can rust on an 'E' type, but with patience, it can be protected by insinuating a probe up inside it, from the bulkhead access plate or sometimes through the hinge apertures.

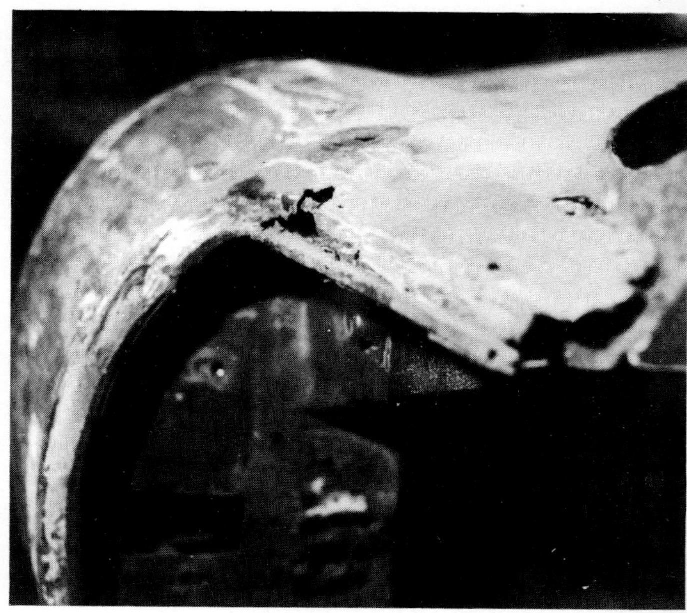

This part of the underside is painted as per the top surfaces of the car, and it's a good idea to stick to this finish, as a thick coating of sealant will only disguise the build up of rust, until it's too late.

The remainder of the car's underside is quite smooth too, though the box members on which the rear suspension sub-frame is mounted can sometimes corrode through — during the rear wheelarch cleaning exercise you should have got rid of the mud around the mounting rubbers, and you can also drill one face on each of the three 'angles' and inject with Waxoyl. The last sections to be protected underneath are the square-section box members running lengthwise down the car either side of the prop shaft area. You can either enlarge the gap left where the section was folded over, or drill a new hole. It isn't really necessary to coat the whole underbody with a sealant, because open flat areas don't rot — just clean, inspect and treat seams, joins and cavities on a local basis.

The outside of the E-type is smooth and stream-lined, with few exposed seams to attract rust. But it is as well to squirt Tectyl wherever an accessory or chrome trim part is bolted, around lights and up under bumpers. For less messy but rather less permanant protection, WD 40 can be substituted for the Tectyl or Waxoyl. I use WD 40 on every minor spot-welded seam I can find on the car, especially under the bonnet on the bulkhead — it prevents those terrible red trails of rust which otherwise the salt-laden winter spray provokes.

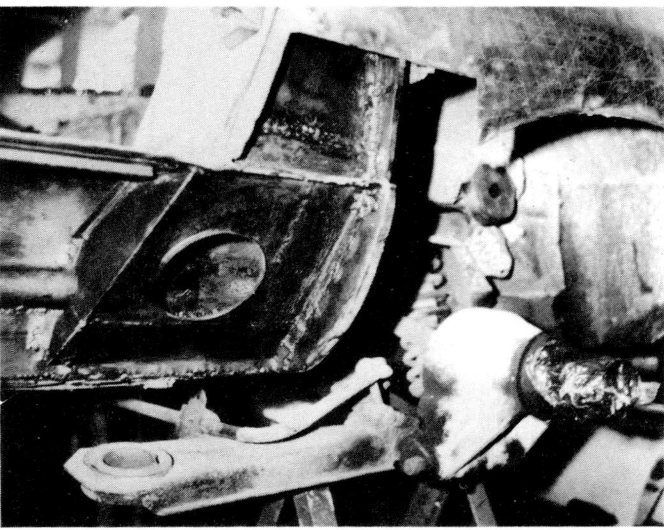

The rear end of the sill, and another plate, this time under the rear door shut pillar and adjacent to the rear wheel arch closing panel. This shows the roadster, which lacks the inner wing which on the fixed-head, arches backwards from top sill level within the wheel arch.

Lastly, there's the doors. The best way to treat these is to remove the door trims completely, as only then can you really ensure that your protective medium is going where it should. Don't forget to spray it upwards as well, as the shoulder of the door has been known to

This is what's behind the 'E' type's outer sill when it's removed. The view here, looking towards the front of the car, shows the flitch-plate which bisects the sill under the front bulkhead, and which prevents fluid simply injected from one end of the sill from doing a proper job — as can be seen, it shields a good area, and where it meets the inner sill at the bottom, forms a neat, water-collecting pocket.

These are the measurements for drilling the sill closing plate ahead of the rear wheel — the placing of these three holes will ensure that your protective fluid will get both sides of that flitch plate shown in the previous picture.

The writer would like to thank MCR Phoenix Automotive Ltd., the E-type restoration people, for facilities provided during the preparation of this article.

This is the door pillar construction of an 'E' type, showing how the outer skin, when in place, very effectively boxes in an outer section, which is without a drain hole. On the roadster as shown here, you can drill into this section from the rear wheel arch, at about the point of maximum curvature and around an inch in from the outside. On the fixed-head, this part of the wheel arch is covered by the inner rear wing, so you either have to try and obtain access via the inside of the car, or drill the door shut plate above or below the striker plate.

Removing the side trim panel on a fixed-head will give access to most of the boxed side and rear areas of the car. When the cubby-hole box is removed, you will be able to reach backwards to protect the vulnerable inner/outer wing join.

The rear bulkhead can be tackled from above by drilling from the top into the part where the radius arm is mounted. This is about 5½ inches in from the side.

It's a good idea to remove the seats and clean off any surface rust on the floor, and to gain further access to the sill — a manufacturing hole can just be seen between spanner and cross-member; this latter too should be drilled and injected. Pay special attention to where the floor joins the rear bulkhead; on this Series One fixed-head the leathercloth has been pulled back prior to drilling the bulkhead above the radius arm mounting point.

Rear bulkhead on the 2-plus-2 car — lower, and with easier access to the more vulnerable end sections. The sound deadening cotton-waste should be pulled out before treatment, and stuffed back in afterwards.

Underside view of the radius arm mounting. Factory fitted nylon plug can be seen, inside which is the first of the bulkhead compartments — this can be removed for access, and if desired left off so that any water getting in immediately runs out again. To get at the compartment where the arm is actually mounted, however, requires drilling as explained. Also visible is the strengthening rail parallel to the silencer box; it's unusual for this to suffer too badly from rust, but is worth protecting just the same. The whole area surrounding the radius arm mounting should always be kept free from mud.

rust through. The rear door on fixed-heads, and the roadster's boot lid, also needs to be protected.

To carry out all these measures properly isn't a quick exercise, and unless you have a complete week's holiday to spare, don't attempt to do it all in one go. Limit yourself to one self-contained area and just do that, properly — say, one wheel-arch at a time. Remember that you need to leave the car to dry off after washing it underneath, and aim to apply actual rust killers so that they have overnight to 'cure'. Materials will cost you from £10 - £30, according to how much of the car you have to, or wish to, cover.

Above all, don't think that once done, that's it for good. It is essential to clean-off and retreat an actively used car at least once a year, and to keep the build up of road dirt down, it's a good idea to get into the habit of commencing your ordinary car-washing chore by hosing off the underside first. But your hard work will be extremely worthwhile, because you can reckon that for every pound and every hour spent on the car in this way, you'll have saved maybe £100 in bodywork repairs later on. And that gives you a very secure feeling whenever you have to drive your E-type in the rain!

Spare wheel well under treatment. The material has been allowed to run everywhere, especially along and inside the floor strengtheners, around all seams, and under and round the petrol tank. Screwdrivers have been used to scrape surface rust from seams, which can then be neutralised with Trustan or similar before touching in with paint. Cleaning off follows.

Notes on Tools and Equipment

You might think that an amateur without the high-pressure pumps and injectors of a professional rust-proofing company wouldn't stand a chance of obtaining worthwhile results in his front drive; but to weigh against sophisticated equipment, he has time, a high degree of conscientiousness, and no restrictions to speak of in the amount of material he uses to do the job. Besides which, rust-proofing companies don't generally want to know about vehicles more than a few months old at the most.

The range of equipment is only limited by the ingenuity of the owner, and can vary from simply an old washing-up liquid bottle, to compressed-air pressure pots and metal probes. To begin with the simplest, a length of nylon or plastic tubing with the end blocked and radial holes drilled can be fixed into the top of the aforementioned bottle, and be very effective in squirting Waxoyl into cavities. More easily accessible parts can be sprayed using a simple hand-trigger gun, of the sort bought in gardening shops, though buy a couple because they do become blocked eventually.

Finnigans, the makers of Waxoyl, market a syringe-type applicator which is a bit messy but good for coating larger surfaces. However, some sort of probe is definitely needed for reaching internal sections, and an advance on the washing-up bottle is an adaptation of the pump-up 'Killaspray' garden insecticide unit —detach the standard nozzle and substitute a length of old brake pipe tubing, again blocked (or partially blocked) at the end, and perforated with a ring of holes

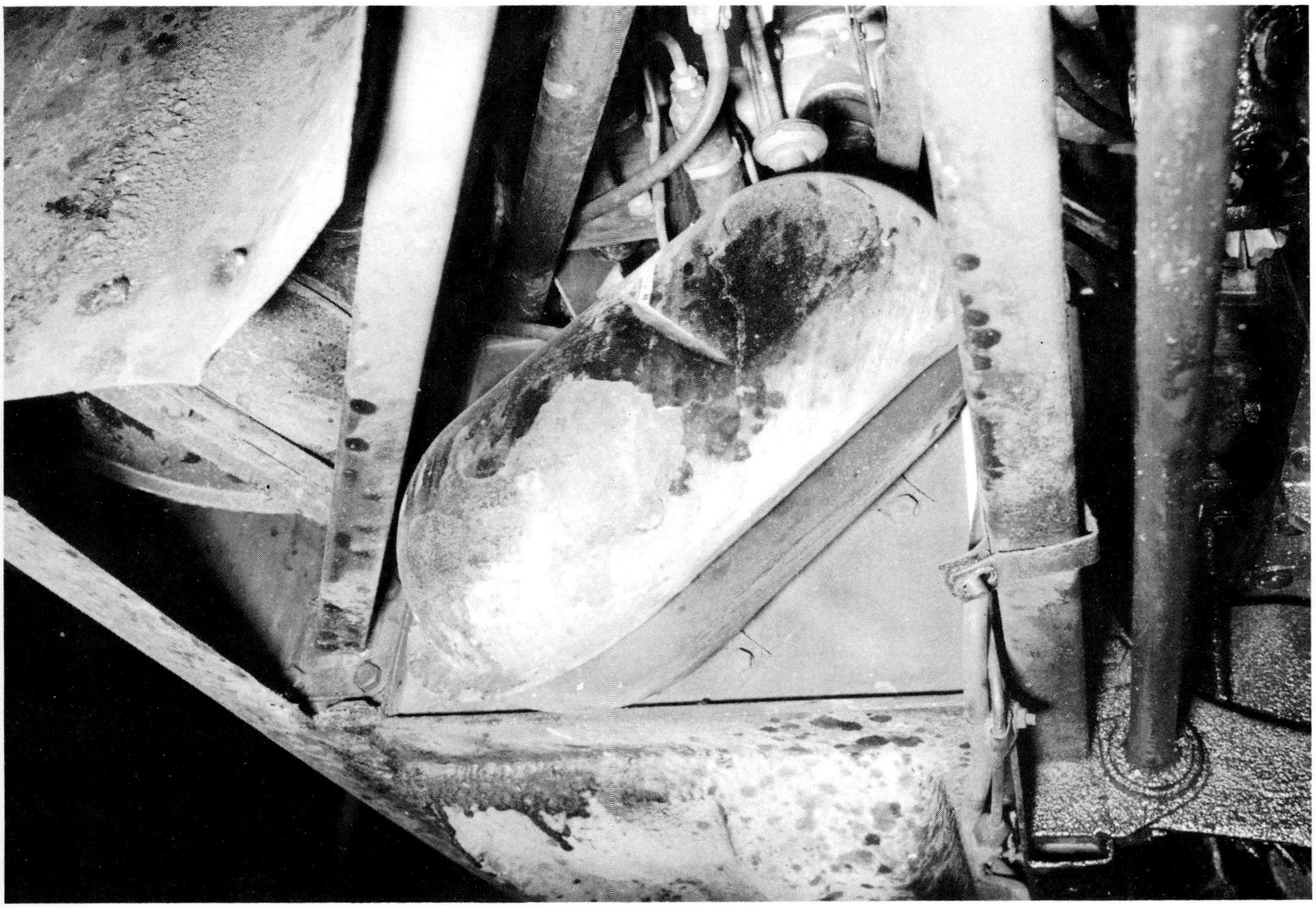

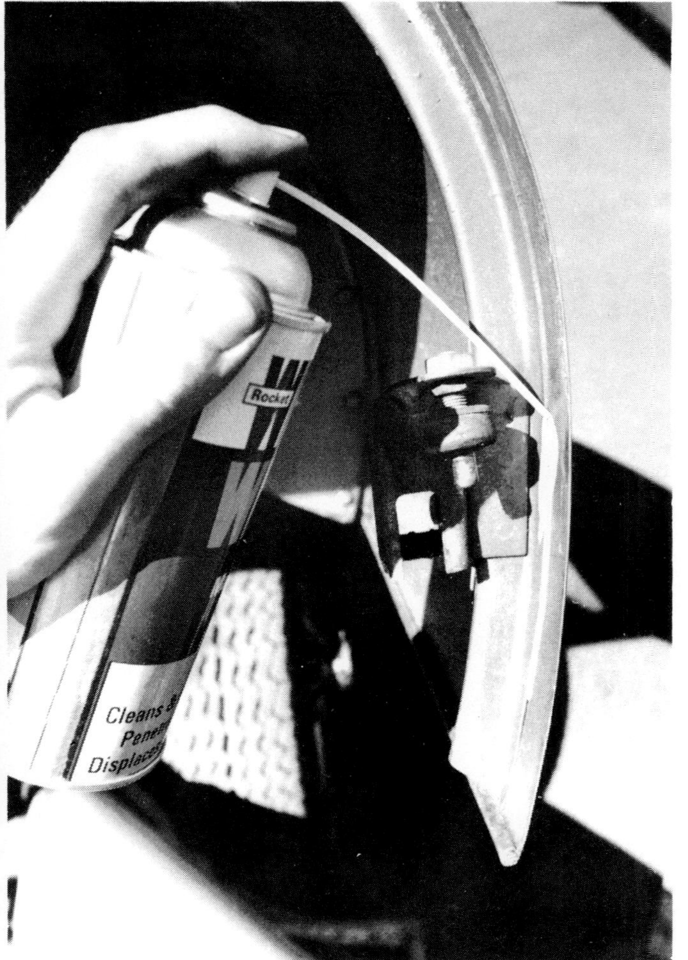

Don't forget areas at the front of the car such as the vacuum reservoir tank which is often forgotten about behind its detachable under panel — and while that's off, clean round the lower frame mounting point too, and around the air cleaner cannister. This is a Series One car of course.

Minor seams and accessory fixtures can be protected with WD40, the excess being wiped off the paintwork after application. This must be repeated every winter though. Attention like this ensures that an 'E' type will continue to be 'new-looking' years after a rebuild.

down the last few inches of its length. Various shapes and angles of probe can be experimented with — and a simple right-angled piece with the end fanned-out to give a spray is very effective when it isn't necessary for a probe to reach several feet inside a cavity.

The Tectyl pack comes complete with a nylon probe which fits on the aerosol — though a tip is to keep all probes in, or partially in, white spirit so that they won't dry out and become blocked.

You should be able to find the Tectyl packs in car accessory shops, though Waxoyl is only available from the makers, at just under £5.00 a gallon. Similar fluids to Tectyl ML and Under Body are marketed by Sound Services of Oxford in gallon cans as 'Rustex'. As prices change, look for the relevent advertisements in 'Thoroughbred & Classic Cars' or 'Exchange & Mart' for up-to-date information and ordering procedures.

Happy squirting!

Jaguar Portfolio

A selection of cars, old and new

The Jaguar 'E' type of 1961 has to be one of the greatest sports car designs of all time — speed and grace combined in a totally usable whole that is a delight to the eye even today. Perhaps the most well known of these cars to JDC members is this example, which has appeared at many of our events during 1978. It is one of the best Series One cars known, and is a 4.2 open two seater, year 1965.

The engine compartment of Bill's 4.2 is almost beyond criticism in its finish; component re-finishing was helped by the fact that the clutch needed replacing, so taking the engine and transmission out meant that underbonnet areas were much more accessible. Yes — it is driven in the rain, as this picture, taken at the club's AGM at the factory, clearly demonstrates — a day which meant a 300 mile round trip in appalling weather.

Its owner Bill Athawes of Purbrook, Hants, bought the roadster in 1975, and it only had 29,000 miles on the clock. So little fundamental work had to be done, although because the car had previously lain unused for six years, the brakes needed overhauling, and the faded paintwork resprayed. Plus, of course, the hundreds of hours of cleaning and detailing which are required for a 'concours' car.

Moment of triumph at Weston Park — Bill pulls in to receive his 'Car of the Day' award from 'Thoroughbred & Classic Cars' magazine, in August 1978; just one of many concours victories, and culminating in the car's display at the Motor Show.

A unique profile, and totally 'Jaguar' — the fixed-head 'E' type. Whitewall tyres were a common option on cars exported to the States (the destination of most 'E' types), but rare in this country. The Series One 4.2 'E' type took over from the 3.8 version in 1964, and evolved into the Series Two car in 1968.

The fixed-head coupe 'E' type is just as beautiful as the open version; this 1965 car also belongs to Bill Athawes, and highlights the original 'E' type's superb lines very well, with the covered headlights and slim bumpers.

After 4.2 came 5.3, and AVV 1 can be heralded as the best in the British Isles. Its owner is Alan Hames from Northampton, and he bought it new in 1972 — for keeps. Again, painstaking attention to detail has made it into the top concours V12 'E' type of 1978, despite four years of every-day use.

Jaguar's first sports car was the SS 100 of 1936, and it possessed no less classic lines than the 'E' type which was to follow many years later. With either a 2½ or 3½ litre engine with an ohv cylinder head designed by the late Harry Weslake, the '100' was amongst the quickest sports car of its day, with the larger engined car able to nudge a genuine 100mph. This 3½ litre belongs to John Owen, is an ex-rally car, and currently is the top 'concours' 100 in circulation.

Perfectly balanced in appearance, the SS 100 embodied all the classic elements of the traditional British sports car. Thus many found their way to the States during the 1950s, though some have since found their way back again. Little over 300 were made, between 1936 and 1939.

Victory! John Owen's SS 100 collects another trophy, this time at the club's Packington Hall meeting.

SS 100 dashboard, with comprehensive instrumentation. The aero-screens were a standard feature, the windscreen folding down 'for speed work'. Riding in an SS 100 is a little bumpy, but even by today's standards, the car is quick off the mark and stable — if old fashioned — round corners.

Now for something completely different. . . There are quite a number of Mk
10 and 420Gs saloons about, not all cherished, and someone had the brilliant
idea of turning them into convertibles. Most projects of this sort turn into a
disaster, but this time, the result seems highly presentable.

Graig Hinton, of Classic Cars of Coventry, had this Mk 10 converted, and
may well go into production with the idea. The shape lends itself surprisingly
well to an open top; the finished item, with fully automatic, electrically
operated hood, would sell for about £4000.

Another 'special', and one almost entirely home built. It belongs to Mr. N.L. Hood of Balsall Common, West Midlands, and uses an XK 150 as its basis — a 1960 car intercepted on the way to the breaker's yard. After stripping and reconditioning the chassis, a full 9:1 3.8 'E' type engine was installed, driving through the original overdrive gearbox, a higher (3.77) rear axle ratio, and Series Three 'E' type chrome wire wheels and tyres.

The original body had been rendered totally useless by rust, so a light aluminium shell of a semi-vintage style was built up on a tubular steel frame. A Mk 10 grille was incorporated into the front of the car, and the usual difficulties of adapting an XK chassis to this sort of coachwork — the forward position of the engine, and the high position of the steering rack which make it awkward to arrive at a pleasant front aspect — have been very well overcome.

Supreme saloon: Gerry Margrave's 420, which this year has won its class in every JDC concours entered, and at the National Classic Car Concours at Weston Park, and the Stoneleigh Show. The car's season was rounded off by being elected Champion of Champions at the club's AGM in October. The car has completed some 90,000 miles but has not been totally rebuilt, which shows that if carefully used, a fairly high mileage shouldn't be a bar to concours victories. Photo: John Williams.

The Jaguar 420 saloon is a successful amalgum of two Jaguar models; it is based on the well-known S-type, which itself is an independent rear suspension version of the well-loved Mk II, but fitted with the 4.2 (instead of 3.4 or 3.8) engine with the 'straight port' cylinder head and two 2-inch SU carburettors. Jaguar all-synchromesh gear-box is standard, or an automatic models, and the combination adds up to a highly driveable, well balanced car.

Rather more out of the ordinary is this Jaguar saloon — it's a modified Series One XJ12, and is one of the fastest road cars in use today. The owner is Harvey Smith (not the horse man!). Wider wheels by Appliance and Pirelli 'P70' tyres are matched by wheelarch flares, while the intakes on the bonnet are functional as they conduct cold air to the carburettors.

With the bonnet up, this impressive sight meets the eyes — six twin-choke Weber carbs, which with gas-flowed heads, re-profiled camshafts and other modifications, hoist the bhp to near 400bhp. Top speed is reckoned to be not far short of 160mph; a four-speed manual gearbox has replaced the standard automatic unit.

Mario Andretti — World Champion, 1978. And we can link him with Jaguar too, if only because of this ride in Geoffrey Stephen's XK 150 drophead at Brands Hatch. The occasion was the British Grand Prix of 1970, when in a parade of XKs celebrating 21 years of XK production, the current GP drivers were driven round the circuit.

Mystery car — number one. Australian Jaguar enthusiasts have been unable to trace the derivation or history of this strange beast. It has an XK engine, but transverse leaf-spring suspension rather like that on a Cooper-Jaguar; bodywork is reminiscent of the big Cunningham Le Mans cars of the mid-fifties.
Photo: Les Hughes

Mystery car — number two. This intriguing prototype is owned by Anthony Taylor of Rishton, near Blackburn, and he'd dearly like to meet the builder or builders of the car. It is beautifully made, using typical Jaguar racing-car methods of construction with the aluminium panelling of the monocoque rivetted together.

The cockpit has been carefully designed, with built-in fresh air ducting which could indicate the builders' intentions of long-distance racing. While it is obviously front-engined, the idea might have been to use a rear 'transaxle' unit, with the gearbox behind the driver. The big sills have an obvious affinity with the 'E' type, and it's thought that the car may have been constructed by Jaguar men in their spare time.

North American enterprise — Bruce Adams with his XKSS replica in course of construction. The bodywork is glass-fibre, and of course Jaguar engine and running gear is used. The shell has been made a little larger than the original, "to have more room inside" — which to those who've ridden in the real thing will realise is quite a good idea!
Photo: Bruce MacLean.

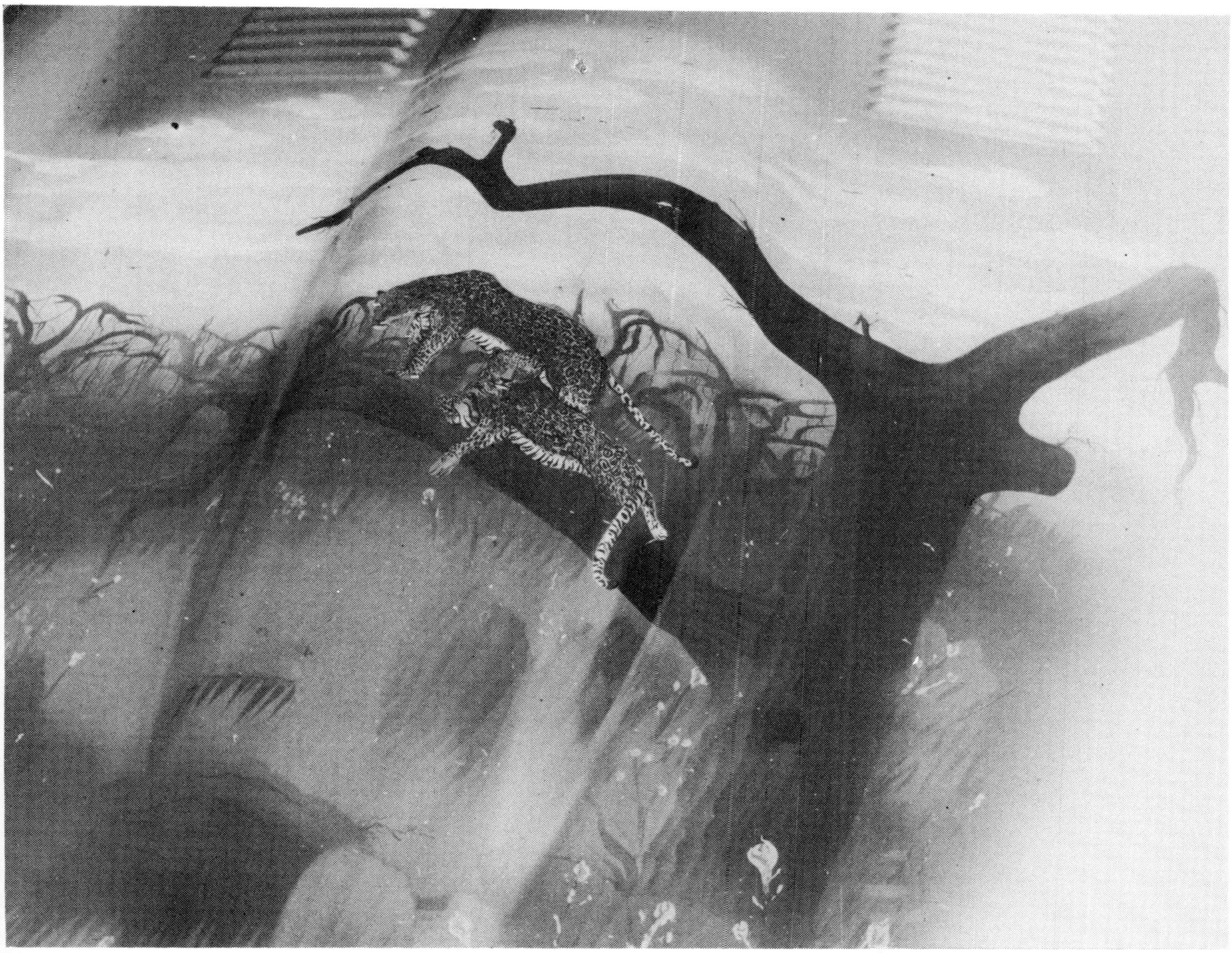

The custom car scene hasn't neglected Jaguar, and besides the widespread use of the Jaguar independent rear end on hot rods, the custom boys have also turned their attention to decorating more or less standard Jaguars. This illustration of 'jaguars at ease' graced the bonnet of an 'E' type seen at a JDC function recently. . .

. . .while this effort, a sort of 'jaguar twilight' illustration, decorated the bootlid of a Mk II saloon.

A 'D' Type at Le Mans

MARTIN MORRIS, elected 1978 'Jaguar Driver of the Year', owns OKV 3, the ex-1954
Le Mans 'D' type, which he and Bryan prepare at their Lakeham Racing business in Devon.
This is his story of the 1978 Historic race at Le Mans where over the full circuit he drove OKV 3
to third place behind Willie Greens long-nose D-type and Stirling Moss's 250F Maserati.
Photographs by kind permission of 'Autocar'.

Martin and OKV 3 head a Lister-Jaguar and C-type on the famous circuit. The D-type was driven in 1954
by Whitehead/Wharton, although it didn't finish.

A superb event for us and the 'D'. We also took the "C" for Hamilton and Rolt to drive in a demonstration run. Took day off Tuesday. Left Tuesday night, via Southampton — Le-Havre. Bryan and Jo in "C". Sue and I in "D" with new special screen for 'the hole'. Remainder of our luggage and spares followed in Michael and Rita's Capri. Lovely weather throughout and a super drive down to Le Mans. Came to an abrupt halt when Gendarmes stopped us with a road block. Told us we had been timed by VASCAR at 170 k.p.h. in 90 limit! Demanded 250 francs *each* = £30 each! We didn't have it, so the flics went off for a conflab. Thinking they'd given up, we re-started engines and were about to drive on when 'our friends' came back at the run, 'hands on holsters!' They said we must follow them to Ern BONK where we must change our money. We duly did so and watched poor Bryan frog-marched in with two Gendarmes on either side. Not content with this, they indicated that we must follow them to the police station where 1½ hours later we emerged,

having filled in numerous forms and confessions, been breathalysed and thoroughly taken to the cleaners.

Arrived Le Mans. Found our White House park. Presented ourselves to Scrutineer and immediately told to go away and fit an external Master switch. Some two hours later, we re-presented ourselves complete with thoroughly dangerous 'live' switch and piece of paper in the cut-out to ensure that it would work/not work when the dynamo is charging. We immediately passed the Scroots who seemed totally disinterested in anything else. Then watched our friends in the '2nd Cinquantenair' complete their practise. Poor Anthony ran a bearing on the Lago Talbot. I was very glad we weren't practising that day, as I was aware of being far from ready.

My next problem was at signing-on where the charming, but efficient, young girl demanded my 'Group Sanguine' — wot's that? Blood group, you clot. Oh, I've no idea. You must have — you've had enough accidents, said my wife. Yes, but I've always been unconscious, you fool. "I MUST see your certified group sanguine". — Oh! — quick think — shall I make one up? No, it seems she's going to demand proof and, anyway, I'm not sure I like the idea of getting the wrong mixture pumped into me in the event of the worse coming to the worst. So I get instructions where to go to the 'Laboratoir'. No, not the Abbatoir.

We found our way via Arnage to our superb auberge on the banks of the Loire, renewing acquaintance of five years before. The aura of peace and quiet was like entering paradise, after the hectic rush and bustle of the journey, the police, the scrutineers and the noise and dust of the circuit.

Next day, we set off for the circuit after lunch and arrived about 3 p.m. to hear my name being paged over the Tannoy. It was my girl-friend at race control who had gone quite neurotic about still not having my confounded blood group. At least I felt I'd kept my 'sang-froid'.

We got ready to practise, and then off we all go, with Stirling Moss away first in the 250 F. I was heartened to learn that he too had been caught for speeding on the way down in his Renault 5TL and the well known advert. "Who do you think you are — Stirling Moss"? had actually come true. We got into our stride down the Mulsanne straight and I was pleased to find my new 3.07 Diff. lovingly selected and supplied by my very good friend at Salisbury's was going to be ideal. We reached 5,700 the first time and then I was going through the kink with a quick change to oversteer as the change of direction coincided with a camber-change. Then we were over the brow and feeling the brakes as Mulsanne corner approached — Wooah — boy, watch it — blast, you blithering idiot, I said to myself, as it rapidly dawned on me that we weren't going to make the hairpin corner. On towards Tours we went in true S. Moss 1953 style. Quickly round, using the grass verge and back with a red face, to see my overtaken friends all sail past before I could find a gap and join them.

The remaining ½-hour practise passed quickly and without incident, with the car going beautifully. I was lifting at 5,800 to save the engine. Brakes quite good and no sign of over-heating, which proved the value of Bryan's beautifully made cooling ducts which he had just the previous weekend fabricated and fitted for me. Once again, I found the new complex of corners from Arnage to the Ford chicane very difficult to learn and get anywhere near right.

That night, I had asked Walter Hill from Miami, Florida, and Chris Keith-Lucas of Lynx Engineering to eat with us at our hotel. I led the way in OKV 3 with Bryan in the hole, while Walter and Chris followed in the "D" which Lynx had very recently bought and Walter had borrowed for the event. After 20 kms or so, we turned off the main road, but Walter seemed to get left behind. We waited, then went back. There they were with the "D" stuck in top gear. Chris was trying to check the gear lever linkage while Walter was saying 'give it a tap with a big rock!' Bryan quickly confirmed Keith's opinion that the problem was 'internal', so we push-started them in 4th gear and carried on to our destination. B & C immediately set to to dismantle the gearbox selector mechanism, with Walter lending support while I had a shower, and a drink. The problem went deeper than could be overcome then, so we agreed to have dinner. Chris and Walter would go back to the circuit that night in the "C".

Next morning dawned as sunny and beautiful as ever, with the swallows dipping in La Loire, the roses on the white painted frontage of the restaurant, and before long, our various wives and girl-friends were stretched out on the green grass with minimal coverage. Walter and Chris arrived early from the circuit full of compliments about the "C" which Walter proclaimed a really great road car, which it is. Bryan and Chris disappeared into the bowels of the "D" gearbox: Walter hovered by it, offering verbal encouragement, while I set to to complete last winter's non-existant re-build and race preparation of OKV 3. Actually, I did have a job to do in changing pads and bleeding the brakes, plus changing a weepy seal in one of my front calipers. It was only by courtesy of Michael and Rita that I had the pads as I had discovered on our day of departure that Ferodo had sent me the wrong ones and an afternoon of frantic telephoning had sent them on their way by Red Star to Plymouth where Michael and Rita could collect them on their crossing via Plymough — Roskoff. What would Martin do without his constantly sponged-upon friends?

Willie Green at full flight in the JCB D-type.

Our car park was already full of exotic machinery — "C" Type, 2 "D" Types, 2 Lagos, Targa Florio Alfa, 4½ Bentley, Testa Rossa, etc., when a great waft of mechanico-musical harmonics heralded the arrival for lunch of a Ferrari club with various examples of Ber inetta, GTO, GTB and so on, including our good friend Christian Bavery in his tatty, but lovely, S.W.B. Lightweight. A marvellous lunch stretched into late afternoon, and Bryan, having sent the mended Walter and Chris happily on their way, told me to snap out of it and take him out to test his re-jetting, re-choking and general 'breathing' on my Webers. We spent an interesting hour frightening chickens, horses and ordinary country-folk, having completed several part-throttle cuts for plug checks. On returning, who should arrive but Duncan Hamilton, with James Tilling (English Le Mans commentator for the last ¼-century) and Duncan's good friend/co-driver-for-getting home, John Knight. I'd invited them to dinner and we spent an evening of escalating hilarity which I shall never forget, but of which I wish I could remember much more. James T. turned out to be a comedian who has missed his vocation, and Duncan was a delight as the evening and the stories grew and grew — and Duncan's eyes twinkled out of his marvellous beard.

Race day, and an early start to the serious business. We found our way to the circuit and 'our' paddock through the swelling crowds. We met up with Tony Rolt who had only flown in during the early hours and had succeeded in navigating himself through 40 miles of country lanes to avoid the jams.

I was just explaining to Tony that I could remove the steering wheel of the "C" to help him get his long legs in and out when I was horrified to see that Duncan had already succeeded in getting behind the wheel and was sitting there grinning like a naughty school-boy. There was much confusion over how, when and where we were to carry out the Demo. which was to be a lap of honour by Duncan and Tony in the "C" to celebrate their great 1953 "C" type win of 25 years ago, when, for the first time, the race was won at an average of over 100 m.p.h. and the famous Dunlop disc brakes were used by Jaguars for the first time ever at Le Mans, and with such devastating success. I was supposed to follow them in Duncan's XJS, specially painted in Ecurie Ecosse blue, with the winners of the two Historic races as my passengers. It didn't quite work out that way, but more in a moment.

We watched the first Historic race — 'the 2 'me Cinquantenaire' — but I don't remember much about it as we were all biting our finger nails in the assembly area. Anyhow, Stephen went really well in 'Talbot'. At last we were allowed out and up to the starting grid between the absolutely packed grandstands. It was very hot and we were allowed no warming-up lap. Stirling was right beside me in the 250F, his mechanics waiting to push-start him into his grid position immediately in front of me. The Start Marshall kept showing us the 3-minutes board, and, of course,

old fool, I'd thought, he's just exaggerating like 211 mph at Agadir. Now I knew who was the fool — criminal maniac more like! as I repeated my first practise lap faux-pas, shot on down the escape road, slewed the car round in a 'U' turn on the grass and waited to join the queue knowing I'd thrown it all away. Actually, I slotted in pretty quickly and soon I found myself behind Richard Bond again. I was quite angry and could only just hang on to him all round the difficult side of the circuit until the Mulsanne straight came up again and OKV 3 just hurtled past him with what felt like 40 mph in hand. This time, and every subsequent time, I religiously followed Duncan's advice, braked even earlier than the usual M.M. — twice as early as anyone else's technique, crawled into Mulsanne corner and turned it all on as soon as I could see the exit. As usual, after an excursion, I found it difficult to get driving smoothly and with any rhythm again, so I was very conscious of being untidy with Richard on my heels. Another lap and I'd lost Richard and was setting my sights on a Lister. It turned out to be Michael Bowler who was driving very hard and it took me a couple of laps to close up on him, but once again, I only needed to show the straight to OKV 3 and we could take a quarter mile off him, as the Lister seemed to reach its maximum while the "D" just went on and on accelerating. By now, the circuit was getting fairly oily and at Arnage, where I had spun 5 years ago,

Vic Norman in the ex-Ecurie Ecosse D-type leads a contingent of history during the 1978 retrospectif event.

no one started their engines, least of all Stirling, for fear of over-heating. Eventually we were shown a 2-mintes board, and after a leisurely pause, the 250F was fired up. Instantly the Starter held up his flag and dropped it. We were off! Like most of us, I was still pressing my starter button. Away we went and a great heap of us swept up under the Dunlop bridge, through that superb first bend, over the brow and down towards the Esses. I'd passed Moss but he took me and so did John Harper in his Lister Jaguar as we braked for the first 'S'. This got me going, so I entered the Mulsanne straight with my boot well and truly in it. As always, OKV 3 responded superbly and 6000 rpm came up in 2nd, 3rd and then 5.8, 5.9 and 6 in top as we powered past several Listers, the Testa Rossa, then Moss in the 250F with at least 15-20 mph margin. Next was John Harper who didn't see me coming and we had to touch the grass (phew!), through the kink, up and over the brow of the hill, and we came alongside the two leading cars as I started to brake. One moment, I was thinking 'terrific, we'll win this race', whilst the next, I realised I'd bogged it all again. The excitement had gone to my head. I'd forgotten my practise and Duncan's advice of the night before — 'Hit the brakes once before you go over the top, just to make sure they're still there and knock the first 20 mph off'. Silly

the oil flags and cement powder were out on every lap. One Lister after another seemed to have expired by the side of the road in various places, and I was sorry to see Walter Hill's green "D" Type stopped half-way down the straight. As I entered the start/finish area, a Marshal gave me an armfall signal which I took to mean we had finished. I slowed down, dropped my goggles and started to tour round on my slowing down lap. All of a sudden I saw Mike Bowler approaching at break-neck speed in my mirror, and I realised that we could be still racing. Once more, I asked my superb engine to go to and hold 6000 revs. We completed the lap just ahead of Michael and toured round together, with so many waves and cheers that I wondered what all the fuss was about, not knowing if we were within the first ten.

I knew the "C" and XJS had gone on to the start area, so I ignored the Marshal's waving me back into our paddock and drove on and up the Pits road. There was a fantastic crowd of spectators plainly mobbing the winners and no signs of the "C" or the "S". I strolled back to the centre of the mob to see Stirling and Willie wreathed in flowers, girls and champagne. They greeted me with a shout and I was hauled up on to the Dias, given a wreath and swig from Stirling's cup and told I was third! Great.

The 1978 Le Mans historic festivities were partly to celebrate Tony Rolt and Duncan Hamilton's famous 1953 win for Jaguar in a C-type. Here they are about to lap the circuit again in Martin Morris's C-type.

I walked back to the "D" as soon as the mob subsided a bit, to find consternation amongst the 24-hour pit crews and Marshals who were trying to push it away and quite unable to get her out of 1st gear having been foiled by the inter-lock.

Next moment, the XJS arrived, driven by a delighted Michael Scott who, in characteristic manner, had acquired two blondes (Sue and Amanda Bond) as passengers. He immediately acquired my bottle of champagne and we set off once again round the circuit. We paused to commiserate with Bobby Bell, then we were flagged down by a highly excited Walter. We swapped cars so that Walter could drive OKV 3 and I the XJS. Then Michael and Walter swapped places. Michael was over the moon and reckoned he must be the first person to have driven an XJS down the Mulsanne straight, with two blondes, whilst swigging champagne.

We returned to the paddock. I parked OKV 3 with her garland of carnations, chatted to our various friends to find out how everyone had fared, had a lovely picnic lunch with far too much wine, then we all strolled off in a haze to watch the start of the 24-hours.

The Renaults were quite impressive.

The remainder of the afternoon is a bit hazy. We walked for a long time with Stephen Grisewold and Rita and Michael Wilson, around the circuit and 'the village'. The latter is the most fantastic mixture of fair, carnival, side-shows, eating places of all Nationalities, strip-tease, freaks, camps, and, occasionally motor racing. The highlight was the 'cooked in front of you' pancakes with Grand Marnier! As night falls, the whole world takes on an aura of magic, with the great wheels and dippers, switch-backs, music and coloured lights and people and the Goodyear Balloon with its trailing tail showing the positions of the racing cars, and all the while in the background, there is the howl of racing engines going on and on for ever. When you go to the circuit edge to see the sweeping head-lights, you realise how incredibly fast and serious is the real world of motor racing, while the unreal world of the 'civilians' is cramming its mouths with toffee apples and candy floss. We went to the Esses and watched in amazement for three parts of an hour. Then back to the village for an excellent meal, then to the pits to see the frantic work of a wheels, fuel and pads change for a Porsche. Finally we bade goodnight to poor Stephen Grisewold who had nowhere to go for the night, while we found our way back to the White House Park where OKV 3 was waiting by the little Lynx Caravette of Walter Hill and Chris K-L. We joined them for a 'cuppa', and then set off back to our hotel. I had never even lifted the bonnet of my marvellous "D" type to check water or oil or change back to road plugs. I knew there was no need.

The rest of this story is of interest to the writer but boring for the reader. We saw the end of the race on Sunday and returned home on Monday. We visited our French Vintage car friends at Caen who gave us such a good lunch that we missed our boat at Cherbourg!

It was a good week.

Overseas Jaguar Clubs

While the JDC has informal 'centres' overseas, most countries have their own Jaguar clubs, and owners living there are urged to make contact with their home organisation — though we are delighted to welcome enthusiasts of all nationalities into the JDC, to join the many hundred already enrolled. Here, we list the major Jaguar clubs known to us, but for up-to-date information, and if no reply is received from any of these addresses, contact JDC HQ in London.

UNITED STATES

Virtually all Jaguar clubs in North America are organised on a regional basis, and are affiliated to Jaguar Clubs of North America, Inc. As there are over 40 of them, and secretaries' addresses change, write to Fred Horner at JCNA, 600 Willow Tree Road, Leonia, New Jersey 07605 for the address of the one nearest you.

However, a few North American Jaguar clubs are organised on a more international basis, and publish fine monthly or quarterly journals of universal interest. The Classic Jaguar Association comes into this category, with its bias towards older, SS Jaguars. Membership chairman is Richard J. Zolla, 1138 Dorset Lane, Costa Mesa, Calif. 92626. Then the Atlanta Jaguar Society, PO Box 53345, Atlanta, Georgia 30355, also publishes an impressive quarterly magazine which is obtainable on subscription to all.

The Eastern Jaguar Automobile Group (EJAG) must also be mentioned, although not affiliated to the JCNA. 'EJAG News' is circulated monthly and contains much valuable information on Jaguar matters, particularly on the practical side. Write to Box J., Carlisle, Massachusetts 01741.

BRAZIL

Jaguar Driver's Club of Brazil, W.G. Halberstadt, Rua Haddock Lobo, 281-Apt. o 122, Sao Paulo-Sp-01414, Brazil.

AUSTRALIA

Jaguar Driver's Club of Australia (New South Wales), PO Box 2, Drummoyne, NSW 2047.

Jaguar Driver's Club of Southern Australia, PO Box 30, Rundle St, Adelaide, SA 5001. .

Jaguar Car Club of Victoria, Box 161, Ringwood, Victoria 3134.

Jaguar Car Club of Tasmania, PO Box 131, PO, North Hobart, Tasmania 7000.

Jaguar Driver's Club of Canberra, Box 400, Kingston, ACT 2604.

Classic Jaguar Club of Western Australia, 3 Bowen St, Langford, WA 6155.

SWEDEN

Svenska Jaguar-klubben, Box 42092, 126 12 Stockholm 42, Sweden.

SWITZERLAND

Aldo Vinzio, B.P. 34-1211 Geneve 17, Switzerland.

FRANCE

Dr Philippe Renault, 39 Avenue de Laumiere, Paris 19, France.

United States

Rick Zolla, of Costa Mesa, California, is Membership Chairman of the Classic Jaguar Association, and seems to take his camera everywhere! This picture shows the CJA's May 1978 meeting, with Mk Vs, XKs and SS 100s in abundance.

This 1948 3½ litre drop-head is owned by Dr Reese Polesky, and is original and unrestored. The last non-independently sprung Jaguar, these 'Mk IVs' are becoming increasingly sought-after.

Photo: Rick Zolla.

Rick Zolla's own fixed-head 'E' type, with Don Becker's SS 100. As he says, 30 years of tradition.

Devasting line-up of SS 100s; owners are, from left to right, Betty Keith, Don Becker, Hugo Molner, Paul Myers, Holly Hollenbeck, and Jack Rabell. When was the last time we saw this many 100s together in England? *Photo: Rick Zolla.*

The engine compartment of Jack Rabell's 1939 SS 100, looking very 'factory' in presentation. Gone are the days when to win an American concours everything had to be dipped in the plating bath. *Photo: Rick Zolla.*

Mk IIs are appreciated in the States too — this pleasant wire wheeled car was spotted at a Jaguar Owners Club of Los Angeles concours meeting.   *Photo: Rick Zolla.*

Until this year, 1978, when Mario Andretti won the world title, America's only World Champion was Phil Hill, driving for Ferrari. However, Hill commenced his motor racing career on XK 120s, after an MG TC, so was pleased to pose beside Dan Kennedy's XK 150S during the 1976 Laguna Seca Jaguar meeting. Dan (right) has of course been putting the cat amongst the concours pigeons over the past couple of seasons by demonstrating in England what the best American XK restorations are like.

Bob Smiley, who lives at Northport, near New York, bravely took over an old XK 140 racer, and turned it from a rather battered old war-horse to one of the smartest cars in Sports Car Club of America racing. The engine uses expertise from Gran Turiémo Jaguar, and in his first full season, Bob has brought home two first places, three seconds and two thirds.

Photo: Claus Rossin

Inset: Bob's wife Marie designed this display board as part of the XK racing effort, and it was painted up by Karen Miller of the Empire Division Jaguar Club, of which Bob's a member. Not quite visible is the team's motto in Latin, which reads 'Currere Animi Causa'', which Karen hopes is translated as "Run for Fun".

Photo: Karen Miller.

Also in SCCA racing, but at a rather more competitive level, is the 'Gran Turismo Jaguar' 'E' type roadster which has been amazingly successful over the past 12 months in the States. In SCCA racing, cars are divided into classes according to performance, but the 'E' type generally wins overall, beating cars with almost twice the engine capacity. Driver is expatriate Englishman Fred Baker, and as can be seen, both car and driver appear to be quite dwarfed by the dynosaur-like home products.

Fred Horner, who runs the flourishing Jaguar Clubs of North America headquarters in Leonia, New Jersey; there are now some 40 clubs affiliated to JCNA. Fred and his wife came from England, and are familiar and well-loved figures at JCNA events. Here Fred chats to Lisa Clarkson during the First Annual Line Chinetti International Concours d'Elegance in August 1978.

Karen and Ed Miller's superbly restored 1952 XK 120 roadster at the Chinetti Concours. Note that the licence plate depicts model in roman numerals, and the year! *Photo: Claus Rossin.*

XJ in action — Stan Felt winds his 1974 XJ12L round the pylons to win his class in the Gymkhana held by the Empire Division, Jaguar Clubs of North America at Lime Rock. *Photo: Claus Rossin.*

No ordinary E-type this — it's powered by a 350 cu. in. V8 Corvette engine. Pilot is noted Jaguar tuning wizard Al Garz of New York, taking Paul Sabert round Lime Roack during Empire Division's weekend at the track. *Photo: Claus Rossin.*

Another Gymkhana class winner at Lime Rock: Cliff Neely's XK 120 roadster being put through its paces.
Photo: Claus Rossin.

XK drag: part of Empire Division's Lime Rock weekend consisted of timed ¼-mile sprints. Here a match race between two XK 120s is about to begin, with Virgil Caruso's roadster and Jim Stetson's fixed-head being flagged away by Charles Lenzinger. *Photo: Claus Rossin.*

Good to see an XJS given its head. Driver Gene Farkas
propelled the car round at a speed sufficient to set a new
Empire Division lap record during the Lime Rock weekend.
Photo: Claus Rossin.

This superb 2-plus-2 V12 E-type belongs to George and Rita
Rhein and is consistently amongst the winners at North
American concours events.

This is Tom Jaycox's superbly prepared 'competition' XK 120, on display at the Classic Jaguar Association's concours at Fort Lee, New Jersey in June 1978.

Photo: Claus Rossin.

Special number plates certainly aren't exclusive to the British. This is Joe Shea's New Jersey XK 150, attending the CJA's Fort Lee gathering. *Photo: Claus Rossin.*

Yes, they have D-types in the States too. This is Dick Willard's car on display. *Photo: Claus Rossin.*

Action again, this time at Floyd Bennet Field, an old airforce base near New York. Scot Grosfield takes his 1971 E-type round the fast and demanding course laid out by Empire Division's organisers. Note the New York skyline!

Photo: Claus Rossin.

Halt in the sun during the autocross on the great expanse of Floyd Bennet Field; in the foreground is Bob Smiley's completely original XK 120 roadster, used on the road when he needs a change from his fiercesome racing XK 140. Jim Stetson's XK 120, Sal Guera's E-type, and Gene Farkas' XJS gather round.

Great discovery! This very early XK 120 roadster was recently found with only 28,600 miles on the clock, by Empire Division's concours organiser Karen Miller. She and husband Ed eventually intend to bring it up to the same sort of standard as their rebuilt 120, but meanwhile Karen has entered some competition events with the car. Here, she is seen with 670293 at Bridgehampton, practicing for the Historic Race at Watkins Glen which was run in conjunction with the US Grand Prix — she finished 12th. *Photo: Paul Sabert.*

Sweden

Certainly, Sweden contains some of the keenest Jaguar enthusiasts, and the 'Svenska Jaguar Klubben' is one of the most active of all Jaguar clubs. This picture illustrates a typical Swedish Jaguar meeting, and demonstrates the variety of cars represented in that country.

Mk IIs are a favourite in Sweden, and are possibly the most numerous type of obsolete Jaguar there.

Secretary of the Swedish Jaguar Club is Bernth Liljegren, who puts an enormous amount of work into the club. We are also pleased to see increasing numbers of our Swedish counterparts visiting Jaguar events in Great Britain. This is Bernth's own XK 120 fixed-head.

Sweden can even boast of having at least one S.S.1 saloon, as evidenced by this very smart example.

The Jaguar Directory

Here is a list of firms and services which may be of help to Jaguar enthusiasts, particularly those running obsolete models. It is divided into two sections, Europe and North America, and those companies who specifically state that they offer an overseas service are indicated. Please note that the inclusion of an entry in this directory does not necessarily imply a recommendation by the Year Book editor or publishers.

We would be glad to add to this list the names of any reputable concerns brought to our attention, so if you have any suggestions please write to the editor c/o the publishers.

JAGUAR SPARES SOURCES AND SERVICES, EUROPE

F.B. Components, 35-41 Edgeway Road, Marston, Oxford. Oxford 724646/7. Jaguar parts, especially rubber mouldings, brake components etc. Mainly post 1961. Special overseas dept. Telex 837367.

G.H. Nolan, 1 St. Georges Way, London SE15. 01-701 2785. Vast stocks of current and obsolete parts. 10% discount for JDC members (personal cash callers).

Burlen Services, Greencroft St., Salisbury, Wilts. 0722-5100. SU agents — carb overhaul kits, SU pumps etc. Also Jaguar XK exhaust systems. Tyres.

Phillips Garage, 103/7 New Canal St., Digbeth, Birmingham B5 5RA. 021-643 0912. Engine recon. units, servicing, repairs, engine spares. Trade/export service.

British Sports Car Centre Ltd, 308, King St., Hammersmith, London W.6. 01-741 3997. E-type parts a speciality, also Mk II & S-type.

Olaf. P. Lund & Son, Tillingham Street Garage, 35 Tillingham St., Sparkbrook, Birmingham 12. 021-772 2655. New and secondhand parts for most models.

Midland Car Restorations, 1-5 Carver St., Birmingham, B1 3DF. 021-236 2854. XK body restoration & panel work; some XK and Jaguar parts.

Forward Engineering Co. Ltd, Kenilworth Road Garage, Hampton in Arden, Warwicks. Hampton in Arden 2163. Exchange engines and all mechanical work. Engine dynometer & rolling road service. Tuning and racing preparation for road & track. Discount to JDC members.

J. Stock, 71 Micheham Down, London N12. Full or part exhaust systems for most Jaguars inc. Mk II, S-type, XK 140/150, E-type etc. 01-445 6821.

R. Vincent (Coachworks), 72a Gladstone Road, Boscombe, Bournemouth. Bournemouth 33627. Body and mech. restoration. New & secondhand parts.

SS & L Auto Engineering, Home Farm, Holmlea Road, Datchet, nr Windsor, Berks. Slough 47016. All mechanical work, any Jaguar.

MCR Phoenix Automotive Ltd, 1-5 Carver St., Birmingham B1 3DF. 021-236 2854. Complete E-type restoration, body and mechanical.

Classic Autos, 10 High Street, Kings Langley, Herts. Kings Langley 62994. Body repair specialists, XK 120, 140, 150 & C-type. Some replica parts/body panels for XKs.

Woolies Trim & Accessories, 9a Exeter St., Bourne, Lincs PE10 9NJ. Various trim parts including for early E-types. Leather renovation kits. Overseas service. 07782-2731.

Oldham & Crowther, 27 Ivatt Way, Westwood Industrial Estate, Peterborough. Peterborough 262577/265021/265046. Telex 32398. Large range of Jaguar parts, mechanical, bodywork, trim. Exchange units. Overseas service.

Pieter Zwakman, Stoet 18, St. Maarten, Holland. 02262-2293 or 02246-1080. XK specialist, including replica parts.

Motor Wheel Service Repair Company, 71 Jeddo Road, London W12. 01-743 3532. UK distributors for Dunlop wire wheels; repairs, conversions.

Kimble Engineering Ltd, 33 Highfield Rd., Birmingham, 28 0EV. 021-777 2011. New Jaguar knock-off hub caps. Overseas service.

Queens Motor Factors, Gt. Eastern Road, Sudbury, Suffolk. Sudbury 73525. Jaguar brake parts for most models. Overseas service.

British Auto Spares, St. Aarons, Usk Road, Gaerleon, Gwent. Trim parts for Jaguars inc. carpets. Overseas service. 0633-420608.

Michael Cane Restorations Ltd, Mill Lane, Godalming, Surrey. Godalming 22303. E-type, XK restoration specialists.

Suffolk & Turley, 8 & 20 Charwood Avenue, Nuneaton, Warwicks. Nuneaton (0682) 327939 or 381639. Jaguar retrimming specialists.

D.K. Engineering, 24 Davenham Avenue, Northwood, Middlesex. Northwood 25435. Jaguar restoration & sales.

Phoenix Engineering, Rawcliffe Bridge, Goole, Yorkshire. Goole 83339. E-type specialists — large range of mechanical & body parts. Overseas service and agents.

P.J. Langford & Co., Unit A, Mushroom Farm Trading Estate, Derby Road, Eastwood, Notts. Lanley Mill 69838. Stainless steel exhaust systems.

W & M Fibreglass Products, 18 Dalry Road, Adrossan. Adrossan 61555 (53667 evenings). XJ6 glass fibre panels.

Speedy Cables, 10-12 Gaskin Street, London N1. 01-226 9228. Speedo & rev counter cables, also cables made to pattern. Instrument repair service.

Allied Rubber Products, 93-95 Soho Road, Handsworth, Birmingham BR21 9SR. 021-554 6421/2. Rubber mountings, extrusions, sponges, matting.

Birmingham Safety Glass Co Ltd, Lower Essex Street, Birmingham B5 6SS. 021-622 2114/5. Glass for most Jaguars inc. laminated screens.

D & G Parts (Coventry) Ltd, 16a, Gough's Yard, Coventry Street, Coventry. 0203-455602. New and used spares, esp. Mk II, 10, S-type, XJ.

J.W. Tester, 3 School Road, Byfield, Daventry, Northants. Mechanical work, including racing engines, suspension etc.

Lakeham Racing, Lakeham House, Higher Ashton, Exeter, Devon. 0647-52248. Mechanical work, C-type, D-type race preparation etc.

Deetype Replicas Ltd, South Gibcracks Farm, Bicknacre Road, East Harringfield, Chelmsford, Essex. D-type replicas etc.

CHROME PLATING:-

T. Smith & Co., 35 Clerkenwell Close, London EC1. 01-253-7314

London Chroming Co., 26 Sequoia Park, Hatch End, Middx. 01-428-1031

Ducalex (Platers) Ltd. Knightcott Trading Estate, Banwell, Weston-Super-Mare. Banwell 2512. Restoration of rad. cowls, bumpers etc..

DBT Chrome Plating, Mercantile House, 99-101 St. Leonards Road, Windsor, Berks. Windsor 57349

BEAD BLASTING, SHOT BLASTING ETC:-

On site Blasting, London. 01-578-3810

Forge Ahead Products, Lower Fore Street, Exmouth. Exmouth 73775. Also turning, welding etc.

Warren James, Upton-on-Severn (Worcs) 2119. Mobile impact finishing.

Impact Finishers Ltd. Ajax Avenue, Slough, Berks. Slough 26511. Bead & other types of blasting, plus zinc & aluminium spraying etc.

JAGUAR SPARES SOURCES AND SERVICES, NORTH AMERICA

Moss Motors Ltd, 7200 Hollister Avenue, PO Box MG, Goleta, California 93017. Large inventory, especially XK, including reproduction items. Phone 800 235-6954

Vintage Jaguar Spares (Robert C. Brosen), 7804 Billington Court, Oxon Hill, Maryland 20022. 301-248-6327. Especially SS, Mk V, XK.

Bassett's Restorations & Supplies, PO Box 145, Peace Dale, R.I. 02883. Information: 1-(401)-789-1709. Many reproduction items, trim, mechanical, body etc for XK and other Jaguars.

Jaguar Farms, Jack H. Rabell, 2860 W. Victoria Drive, Alpine, Calif. 92001. (714) 445-3152. Mk V and SS spares.

XKs Unlimited, 4420 Edna Rd, San Luis Obispo, Calif. 93401. (805) 544-7864. Reproduction items and n.o.s. used parts.

F&R Import Ltd, 2300 West Hampden Avenue, Englewood, Colo. 80110. 761-5806. Parts and repairs.

Bruce MacLean, 21 Park Ave., Venice, Ca. 90291. (213) 392-4308. Parts for older Jaguars, tuning of pre-1968 Jaguars.

Dayton Wheel Products, Inc., 2326 E. River Rd, Dayton, Ohio 45439. 513-294-2606. Restoration of wire wheels, plating, refinishing, spokes made to order, etc.

Imparts Ltd, 2535 S. Brentwood Boulevard, St Louis, Mo. 63144. (314) 962-0810. Large selection Jaguar parts, inc. XK. Exhaust systems, electrical etc.

Bill Hirsch, 396 Littleton Ave., Newark, N.J. 07103. (201)-243-3858. Convertible tops (from 1952), carpet material, leather, etc.

Bill Tracy, 3179 Woodland Lane, Alexandria, Virginia 22309. 703-360-6652. New and used spares, Jaguar reproduction items. XKs a speciality.

The English Car Company, 850 Government Street, Mobile, Alabama 36602. 1-205-433-0385. Parts and service, Jaguar specialist.

Jag Spares (Walt Osborn), PO Box 140, Tempe, Arizona. (602)-966-6578. Reproduction & replacement parts.

English Car Spares Ltd, 1238 Fernwood Circle N.E., Atlanta, Georgia 30319. (404) 233-1917. Used parts especially.

Long's British Parts Ltd, Box 19832, K.c., Mo. 64141. Original and reproduction parts, XK to XJ, inc. rubber door trim etc.

MODEL	INTRODUCED	DISCONTINUED	CHASSIS NO.	NO. BUILT
S.S.1. 2054cc/2552cc (16/20hp)	Oct. 1931	1933		
2054cc: wheelbase 9'4''; wheel diam 18''; bhp 48 at 3600; max speed 71 mph. *2552cc: as above except; bhp 62 at 3600; max speed 75 mph.*				
S.S.II 1052cc	Oct 1931	1933		
Wheelbase 7'7''; wheel diam 18''; bhp 28 at 4000; max speed 60 mph.				
S.S.I 2143cc/2663cc (16/20hp)	Sep. 1933	1936	247001	
2143cc: wheelbase 9'11''; wheel diam 18''; bhp 53; max speed 72 mph. *2663cc: as above except: bhp 68 at 3600; max speed 77 mph.* *Body revised to include full wings and running boards.*				
S.S.II 1343cc/1601cc (10/12hp)	Sep. 1933	1936	306001	
1343cc: wheelbase 8'8''; wheel diam 18''; bhp 37 at 4000; max speed 61 mph. *1601cc: as above except bhp 38 at 4000; max speed 64 mph (estimated).*				
S.S.I Airline 2143cc/2663cc (16/20hp)	1934	1936	In S.S.I series	
See S.S.I. *Based on S.S.1 chassis with 'fastback styling and twin spare wheels mounted in wings.*				
S.S.I DHC 2143cc/2663cc (16/20hp)	1935	1936	In S.S.I series	105
S.S.90 2663cc sv	Mar. 1935	Nov. 1935	In S.S.I series	23
First Jaguar sports car. *Wheelbase 8'8''; wheel diam 18''; bhp 70 at 3600 approx; max speed 89 mph.*				
SS Jaguar 100 2½ litre (2663cc OHV)	Sep. 1935	1940	18001 ('36-'37) 49001 ('38-'40)	125 65
Wheel base 8'8''; wheel diam 18''; bhp 102 at 4600; max speed 94 mph. *New overhead valve cylinder head by Harry Weslake.* *Similar bodywork to S.S.90.*				
SS Jaguar 1½ (1608cc SV)	Sep. 1935	1937	Chassis no. sequence changed according to year	
SS Jaguar 2½ (2663cc OHV)	Sep. 1935	1937		
Wheelbase 9'11''; wheel diam 18''; bhp 60 at 4500 approx; max speed 70 mph.				
SS Jaguar 100 3½ litre (3845cc)	Sep. 1937	1940	39001	118
Wheelbase 8'8''; wheel diam 18''; bhp 125 at 4250; max speed 101 mph.				

MODEL	INTRODUCED	DISCONTINUED	CHASSIS NO.	NO. BUILT
SS Jaguar tourer 2663cc OHV	Sep. 1935	1937	19001	125

Wheelbase 9'11''; wheel diam 18''; bhp 104 at 4500; max speed 88 mph approx.

Based on 1935 saloon chassis.

MODEL	INTRODUCED	DISCONTINUED	CHASSIS NO.	NO. BUILT
SS Jaguar saloon range — adoption of all-steel bodywork & introduction of drophead coupes	Sep. 1937	1940		

1½ litre 1776cc: wheelbase 10'; wheel diam 18''; bhp 65 at 4600; max speed 71 mph.
2½ litre 2663cc: wheelbase 10'; wheel diam 18''; bhp 102 at 4600; max speed 90 mph approx.
3½ litre 3485cc: as above except; bhp 125 at 4250; max speed 95 mph.

MODEL	INTRODUCED	DISCONTINUED	CHASSIS NO.	NO. BUILT
1½ litre Saloon	20th Nov. 1945	Mar. 1949	410001	5750
2½ litre Saloon			51001	1850
3½ litre Saloon			RHD: 61001	4400
			LHD: 63001	(includes DHC)

Pre-war range continued with minor changes. Specification as above.

MODEL	INTRODUCED	DISCONTINUED	CHASSIS NO.	NO. BUILT
2½ litre Drophead Coupe	24th Feb. 1948	Mar. 1949	527001	
3½ '' '' ''			627001	See above

Specifications as above.

MODEL	INTRODUCED	DISCONTINUED	CHASSIS NO.	NO. BUILT
Mark V 2½ litre Saloon and Drophead Coupe	1st Oct. 1948	Dec. 1950	520001	1661
			54001	29

2663cc: wheelbase 10'; wheel diam 16'';
bhp 102 at 4600; max speed 87 mph approx.
Note: Mk V was first Jaguar to have independent front suspension.

MODEL	INTRODUCED	DISCONTINUED	CHASSIS NO.	NO. BUILT
Mark V 3½ litre Saloon and Drophead Coupe	1st Oct. 1948	Jun. 1951	620001	7831
			640001	972

3485cc: as above except; bhp 125 at 4250;
max speed 91 mph approx.
Mk V was the last Jaguar saloon to be offered with drophead bodywork.

MODEL	INTRODUCED	DISCONTINUED	CHASSIS NO.	NO. BUILT
XK 120 Open 2 Seater  *3442cc; wheelbase 8'6''; wheel diam 16''; bhp 160 at 5000; max speed 120 mph. First Jaguar with OHC XK engine.*	22nd Oct. 1948	Sep. 1954	660001 670001	7,612
Mark V II Saloon  *3442cc: wheelbase 10'; wheel diam 16''; bhp 160 at 5000; max speed 101 mph. Car was termed Mk VII because Bentley had already used 'Mk VI' designation.*	17th Oct. 1950	Sep. 1954	710001 730001	31,000 (all types)
XK 120 Fixed Head Coupe  *Specification as for open 2 seater. From Aug 1951, 180 bhp 'Special equipment' engine available for XKs.*	2nd Mar. 1951	Sep. 1954	669001 679001	2,678
XK 120 'C' Type  *Production C-type: wheelbase 8'; wheel diam 16''; bhp 200 at 5800; max speed 143 mph.*	19th Jun. 1951	Sep. 1954	XKC001	54
XK 120 Drophead Coupe  *Specification as for open two seater.*	18th Apr. 1953	Sep. 1954	667001 677001	1,765
'D' Type  *Production D-type 3442cc: wheelbase 7'6½''; wheel diam 16''; bhp 250 at 5750; max speed 162 mph approx. Later 'works' cars had 3781cc engines developing 270 bhp.*	3rd Sep. 1954	Feb. 1957	XKD401	62
Mark VII 'M' Type Saloon *As for Mk VII except bhp 180 at 5300; max speed 102 mph.*	1st Oct. 1954	Oct. 1956	722755	See Mk VII

MODEL	INTRODUCED	DISCONTINUED	CHASSIS NO.	NO. BUILT
XK 140 Open 2 Seater	15th Oct. 1954	Feb. 1957	800001 810001	3,354

*As for XK 120 except: bhp 190 at 5500 (standard)
or 210 at 5750 (special equipment C-type head);
max speed 125 mph.*

XK 140 Fixed Head Coupe			804001 814001	2,808

*As for open two seater except:
max speed 129 mph (special equipment).*

XK 140 Drophead Coupe			807001 817001	2,889

As for fixed-head.

2.4 litre Saloon	28th Sep. 1955	Sep. 1959	900001 940001	20,000

*2483cc: wheelbase 8'11¼''; wheel diam 15'';
bhp 112 at 5720; max speed 101 mph.
2.4 litre was first Jaguar with unitary bodywork construction.*

Automatic Transmission on Mark VII 'M' for U.K.	Sep. 1955	Oct. 1956	RHD: 727310	

Mark V III Saloon	11th Oct. 1956	Oct. 1958	760001 780001	6300

*As for Mk VII except: bhp 210 at 5500;
max speed 106 mph. B-type head used.*

Automatic Transmission on XK 140 Fixed Head Coupe and Drophead Coupe	Oct. 1956	Feb. 1957	RHD: 804779 RHD: 807475	

MODEL	INTRODUCED	DISCONTINUED	CHASSIS NO.	NO. BUILT
XK 'SS'	30th Jan. 1957	Feb. 1957		16
Specification as for production D-type except; max speed 149 mph.				
XK 150 Fixed Head Coupe (3.4)	22nd May 1957	Oct. 1961	824001 834001	3,445
Specification as for XK 140 except: max speed 124 mph (special equipment). B-type head used on standard 190 bhp cars.				
XK 150 Drophead Coupe (3.4)			827001 837001	1,903
As for fixed-head. XK 150 was first Jaguar road car to be fitted with disc brakes as standard.				
2.4 wider grille (Disc brakes, wire wheels Automatic Transmission optional)	Sep. 1957	Sep. 1959	907974	
3.4 (Disc brakes, wire wheels optional)	Sep. 1957	Sep. 1959	970001 985001	17,350
As for 2.4 except: bhp 190 at 5500; max speed 119 mph. Disc brakes standardised by 1959 Automatic transmission optional.				
XK 150 Open 2 Seater (3.4)	28th Mar. 1958	Oct. 1961	820001	1,297
XK 150 'S' Open 2 Seater (3.4)	*250 bhp at 5500; max speed 132 mph.*		("T" Prefix)	888
Mark IX Saloon	8th Oct. 1958	Sep. 1961	770001 790001	10,000
Specification as for Mk VIII except 3781cc; bhp 220 at 5500; max speed 115 mph. Disc brakes fitted.				
XK 150 'S' Fixed Head Coupe (3.4)	18th Feb. 1959	Oct. 1961	T824789	199
XK 150 'S' Drophead Coupe (3.4)	*See 3.4S Open Two Seater*		T827336	104
Mark II 2.4 Litre Saloon	2nd Oct. 1959	Sep. 1967	100001 125001	30,600
Specification as for 'Mk I' 2.4 except; bhp 120 5750; max speed speed 102 mph.				
Mark II 3.4 Litre Saloon	*As above except: bhp 210 at 5500; max speed 120 mph.*		150001	31,450
Mark II 3.8 Litre Saloon	*As above except: bhp 220 at 5500; max speed 125 mph.*		200001	30,510

MODEL	INTRODUCED	DISCONTINUED	CHASSIS NO.	NO. BUILT
XK 150 Open 2 Seater (3.8)	2nd Oct. 1959	Oct. 1961	820056	42
	As 3.4 except: bhp 220 at 5500;			
	max speed 134 mph (approx.)			
XK 150 Fixed Head Coupe (3.8)	*As open two seater.*		825041	656
XK 150 Drophead Coupe (3.8)	*As open two seater.*		827467	586
XK 150 'S' Open 2 Seater (3.8)	2nd Oct. 1959	Oct. 1961	—	36
XK 150 'S' F.H. Coupe (3.8)	*As 3.8 except: bhp 265 at 5500;*		—	150
XK 150 'S' D/h. Coupe (3.8)	*max speed 136 mph.*		—	89
Power Steering available on	9th Sep. 1960	—	P153037	
3.4 and 3.8 Mark II		—	P202207	
Reclining seats available on				
all Mark II Saloons				
'E' Type Open 2 Seater (3.8)			850001	7,827
			875001	
	3781cc; wheelbase 8'; wheel diam 15'';			
	bhp 265 at 5500; max speed 145 mph.			
'E' Type Fixed Head Coupe (3.8)	15th Mar. 1961	Oct. 1964	860001	7,669
			885001	
	As for open 2 seater except;			
	max speed 148 mph.			
Mark X Saloon (3.8)	12th Oct. 1961	Oct. 1965	300001	13,000
			350001	
	3781cc; wheelbase 10'; wheel diam 14'';			
	bhp 265 at 5500; max speed 118 mph.			
Competition Lightweight 'E'	Mar. 1963	Jan. 1964	S850659	12
	All alloy body; alloy-block engine up to 340 bhp.			
3.4 Litre 'S' Model	10th Sep. 1963	Sep. 1968	1B.1001	11,050
			25001	
	3442cc; wheelbase 8'11½''; wheel diam 15'';			
	bhp 210 at 5500; max speed 118 approx.			
	Car based on Mk II but with indenpendent rear suspension.			
3.8 Litre 'S' Model	*As above except 3781cc; bhp 220 at 5500; max speed 121 mph.*		1B.50001	15,150
			75001	
4.2 Litre 'E' Type Open 2 Seater	9th Oct. 1964	Sep. 1968	1E.1001	9,548
			1E.10001	
	As for 3.8 E-type except 4235cc.			
	External appearance unchanged but new			
	interior, all-syncgro gearbox, new brake servo etc.			

MODEL	INTRODUCED	DISCONTINUED	CHASSIS NO.	NO. BUILT
4.2 Litre 'E' Type F.H.C.	9th Oct. 1964	Sep. 1968	1E.20001	7,770
As for open 2 seater.			1E.30001	
4.2 Litre Mark X	9th Oct. 1964	Sep. 1966	1D.50001	10,550
As for 3.8 Mk X except 4235cc; max speed 121 mph.			1D.75001	(includes 420G)
All synchro-gearbox standard on 'S' models	Mar. 1965	—	—	
All synchro-gearbox standard on Mark II Models	Feb. 1966	—	—	
4.2 Litre 'E' Type 2 + 2	7th Mar. 1966	Sep. 1968	1E.50001	4,220
As for FHC except; wheelbase 8'9''; max speed 148 mph.			1E.75001	
"Ambla" 2.4 Litre Mark II Saloon	5th Sep. 1966	Sep. 1967	120861	
"Ambla" 3.4 Litre Mark II Saloon			171192	
"Ambla" 3.8 Litre Mark II Saloon			235225	
420 Saloon	13th Oct. 1966	Sep. 1968	1F.1001	9,800
As for 3.8S except 4235cc; bhp 245 at 5500; max speed 123 mph. Car based on 'S' saloon with new front end treatment & 4.2 engine.			1F.25001	
420G Saloon	13th Oct. 1966	Aug. 1970	GID.53720	See Mk X
See 4.2 Mk X.			GID.76961	
240 Saloon	26th Sep. 1967	Apr. 1969	1J.1001	
As for 2.4 Mk II except; bhp 133 at 5500; max speed 106 mph. Car based on 2.4 Mk II except straight-port head, Ambla upholstery, new bumpers.			1J.30001	
340 Saloon		Sep. 1968	1J.50001	See Mk II
As for 240 except; bhp 210 at 5500; max speed 120 mph.			80001	
2.8 Litre XJ6 Saloon	26th Sep. 1968	Aug. 1973	1G.1001	
2792cc; wheelbase 9'1''; wheel diam 15''; bhp 180 at 6000; max speed 110 mph approx.			1G.50001	
4.2 Litre XJ6 Saloon			1L.1001	
As for 2.8 except; bhp 245 at 5500; max speed 120 mph.			1L.50001	

MODEL	INTRODUCED	DISCONTINUED	CHASSIS NO.	NO. BUILT
Series 2 'E' Type Open 2 Seater	18th Oct 1968	Sep. 1970	1R.1001 1R.7001	8,627
	Specification as for 4.2 Series One. *Re-styled front with larger mouth, open headlights,* *re-positioned sidelights front and rear.* *Was preceeded by 4.2 car with open headlights* *approx mid-1967 onwards.*			
Series 2 'E' Type F.H. Coupe	*See above.*		1R.20001 1R.25001	4,855
Series 2 'E' Type 2 + 2	*Specification as for 4.2 Series One 2 + 2.* *See above.*		1R.35001 1R.40001	5,326
Series 3 V12 Open 2 Seater	29th Mar. 1971	Sep. 1975	1S.1001 1S.20001	7,990
	5343cc; wheelbase 8'9''; wheel diam 15''; *bhp 272 at 5850; max speed 146 mph.*			
Series 3 V12 2 + 2 Coupe	29th Mar. 1971	Sep. 1973	1S.50001 1S.70001	7,297
	5343cc; wheelbase 8'9''; wheel diam 15''; *bhp 272 at 5850; max speed 142 mph.*			
XJ12	11th Jul. 1972	Aug. 1973	1P.1001 1P.50001	
	As for XJ6 4.2 except 5343cc; bhp 265 at 6000; *max speed 146 mph.*			
XJ6 L XJ12 L	18th Oct. 1972 *As for 'Series One' XJ except wheelbase 9'4¾''*	Aug. 1973	2E.1001 2C.1001	
XJ6 Series 2 XJ6L Series 2	11th Sep. 1973 11th Sep. 1973		2N.1001 2T.1001	

MODEL	INTRODUCED	DISCONTINUED	CHASSIS NO.	NO. BUILT
XJ12L Series 2  *Series 2 V12-engined cars given fuel injection April 1975 to provided greater economy.*	11th Sep. 1973		2R.1001	
XJ6 C Series 2	11th Sep. 1973	1977	2J 1001 2J 50001	
XJ12C Series 2  *As for saloon except wheelbase 9'1''; bhp 285 at 5750; max speed 147 mph. Coupe was only available in UK from April 1975.*	11th Sep. 1973	1977	2G.1001 2G.50001	
XJS  *5343cc; wheelbase 8'6''; wheel diam 15''; bhp 285 at 5500; max speed 153 mph.* *Car is based on XJ saloon floor pan/suspension. Only V12 XJ to be offered with manual transmission.*	10th Sep. 1975		2W.1001 2W.50001	
XJ3.4 *Specification as for XJ6L Series 2 except 3442cc; bhp 161 at 5000; max speed 117 mph. Exterior as XJ4.2L Series 2. Interior has cloth upholstery.*	April 1975		3A.1001 3A.50001	

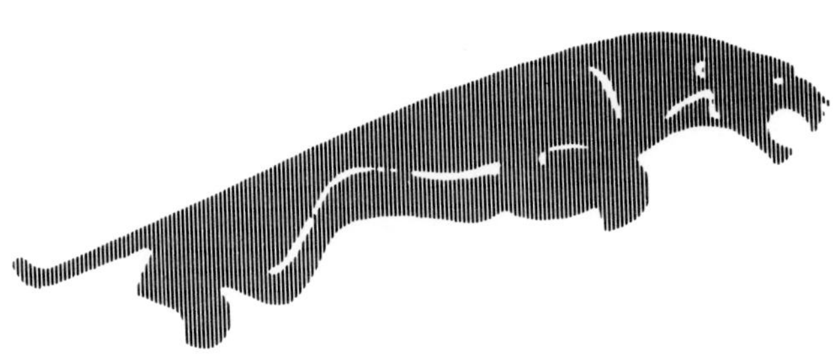

DATES OF INTRODUCTION AND DISCONTINUATION OF DAIMLER MODELS UNDER JAGUAR CONTROL FROM JUNE 1960

	From	To	Commencing Chassis No. (RHD)	No. Built
3.8 Majestic	Jul. 1958	May 1961		
SP 250	4th Apr. 1959	Sep. 1964		
4½ Majestic Major	Oct. 1960	Mar. 1968		
DR 450 4½ Limousine	27th Sep. 1961	Mar. 1968		
Daimler 2½ V8 Saloon	Oct. 1962	Sep. 1967	1A.1001	17,900
Daimler Sovereign (420) Saloon	17th Oct. 1966	Aug. 1969	1A.30001	5,850
Daimler V8 250 Saloon	5th Oct. 1967	Aug. 1969	1K.1001	See 2½
DS 420 Limousine	11th Jun. 1968		1M.1001	
Daimler Sovereign 2.8	9th Oct. 1969	Aug. 1973	1T.1001	
Daimler Sovereign 4.2			1U.1001	
Daimler Double-Six	27th Jul. 1972	Aug. 1973	2A.1001	
Daimler Double-Six Vanden Pl.	26th Sep. 1972	Aug. 1973	2B.1001	
Daimler Sovereign LWB	18th Oct. 1972	Aug. 1973	2D.1001	
Daimler Sovereign Series 2	11th Sep. 1973		2M.1001	
Daimler Sovereign LWB Series 2			2S.1001	
Daimler Double-Six LWB Series 2			2K.1001	
Daimler Sovereign 2-door	Available from April 1975	1977	2H.1001	
Daimler Double-Six 2-door	Available from April 1975	1977	2F.1001	
Daimler Double-Six Vanden Plas Series 2			2P.1001	

Club Calendar

The following is an outline of the Club's official programme for 1979. All Jaguar enthusiasts are welcome to attend.

10 March	Silverstone Race Meeting, Silverstone circuit, nr. Towcester, Northants. For historic cars, plus race for 'standard Jaguars'.
22 April	Sprint Meeting, Curborough, near Lichfield.
5/6 May	XJ Weekend, incorporating XJ Day, tour, dinner dance etc.
20 May	Jaguar Spring Rally, Beaulieu Hants. Big gathering of Jaguars for concours, driving tests etc.
10 June	Yorkshire Jaguar Day, Nostell Priory, nr Wakefield, Yorks.
10 June	Sprint Meeting, Goodwood. Classes for all Jaguars.
8 July	International E-Type Day, Mallory Park, nr Kirkby Mallory, Leics. All Jaguars welcome.
28/29 July	Loton Park Hill Climb, near Shrewsbury. Classes for all Jaguars.
5 August	Southern Jaguar Day, Effingham Park, nr Crawley, Sussex.
16 September	East Anglian Jaguar Day, Banham Motor Museum. (provisional).
23 September	Mk I/II Day, Cliveden House, nr Maidenhead, Berks.
29 September	Annual General Meeting.

Information Desk

All the Club's services:-

JAGUAR DRIVER'S CLUB LTD. HEADQUARTERS
The Norfolk Hotel, Harrington Road, London SW7. Tel: 01-584 9494.
Our full-time staff will be glad to answer your enquiries.

THE REGISTERS

SS REGISTER (Mk V and earlier) Secretary: N.J.B. Drukker, 50 Cross Path, Radlett, Herts. 01-779 5604.
XK REGISTER (XK 120, 140, 150, C- and D-type) Secretary: John Simms, 17 Granville Court, Cheney Lane, Oxford.
MK VII REGISTER (Mk VII, Mk VIII, Mk IX) Secretary: Peter Deffee, 7 Dunstable Road, Caddington, Luton, Beds.
MK II REGISTER (Mk I, Mk II, 240, 340) Secretary: David Webb, 45 Lavender Road, Kempshott, Basingstoke, Hants. Basingstoke 25329.
S-TYPE REGISTER (S-type, Mk 10, 420, 420G) Secretary: John Williams, Ivy Nook, Hamilton Drive, The Park, Nottingham. Nottingham 40347.
E-TYPE REGISTER (6 & 12 cylinder) Secretary: David Nursey, Flat 4, 73 Ravenhurst Road, Harborne, Birmingham B17 9SR.

JAGUAR AREA CENTRES AND REPRESENTATIVES

NORTH HANTS: The Phoenix Inn, West Green, Hartley Wintney, Hants. 3rd Friday in every month.
Area Rep: Daven Uren, 102 Sunny Bank Road, Farnborough, Hants. (AREA 1)
SUSSEX: The Anchor Inn, Barcombe, Nr. Lewes, Sussex. 3rd Tuesday in the month.
Area Rep: C.D. Bovet-White, resident. Tel: Barcombe 400414. (AREA 2)
WEST ESSEX: Plume of Feathers, Pye Corner (on A414) between Harlow and Sawbridgeworth, Essex. 2nd Tuesday in the month.
Area Rep: Mick Davey, 21 Devonshire Road, Walthamstow, London E17. (AREA 3)
KENT & S. LONDON: Sir Thomas Wyatt, London Road, Allington, Maidstone, Kent. 1st Monday in the month
Area Rep: Rick Reading, 47 Acorn Grove, Ditton, Maidstone, Kent. (AREA 4)
DEVON: The Diggers Rest, Woodbury Salterton, Devon. 1st Thursday in the month.
Area Rep: Roy Richards, The Bungalow, Buller Road, Crediton, Devon. Tel: Crediton 2375. (AREA 5)
SURREY/W. LONDON: Moore Place, (The Silk Bar) Esher, (on A3). 2nd Friday in the month. Area Rep: John Pearce, 17 Kevan Drive, Send, Surrey. Guildford 223677. Mark Charles, 22 Garrick Close, Walton-on-Thames. (AREA 6)
MIDLANDS/B'HAM/COVENTRY: The Manor Hotel, Meridon, Warwicks. 1st Wednesday in the month.
Area Rep: Peter Whurr, 12 The Longlands, Barnt Green, B'ham B45 8NY. Tel: 021-445 2618. (AREA 7)
SOMERSET: The Slab House Inn (B3139) near Wells. Last Monday in the month.
Area Rep: Richard Jeanes, Perry Mill Farm, Nether Stowey, Nr. Bridgwater, Somerset. Tel: Nether Stowey 313. (AREA 8)
S. HANTS/DORSET: The Compton Arms, on A31, 1 mile west of end of M27 at Cadnam, Hants. 2nd Thursday in month.
Area Rep: Susan Sommerin, Robin Cottage, Pauls Lane, Sway, Lymington, Hants. Tel: Sway 2839. (AREA 9)
W. SCOTLAND: The Grosvenor Hotel, Great West Road, Glasgow. 1st Tuesday in the month.
Area Rep: Bob Kerr, Luss, Loch Lomond, Dumbartonshire, Scotland. Tel: 664. (AREA 10)
N. YORKSHIRE: Wainstones Hotel, Helmsley Rd., Gt. Broughton, Nr. Stokesley, Yorkshire. 1st Tuesday in the month.
Area Rep: Maurice Lovell, 33 Saunton Rd., Billingham, Cleveland. (AREA 11)
E. SCOTLAND: Royal Scot Hotel (Edinburgh Bar) Glasgow Road, Edinburgh. 1st Thursday in the month.
Area Rep: Jonathan Sheard, 40 Braid Crescent, Edinburgh EH10 6AU. Tel: 031-447 4626. (AREA 12)
CAMBRIDGE: Station Hotel, Great Chesterfield, Essex.
Area Rep: Mac Rutherford, 'Sunrise', 20 Boxworth End, Swavesey, Cambs. Tel: Swavesy 3082 to confirm date. (AREA 13)
GLOUCESTER: The Flying Machine, Brockworth, Nr. Gloucester. 1st Monday in the month.
Area Rep: J. Cookson, Gables Farm, Badgeworth Lane, Cheltenham. (AREA 14)
CHESHIRE: 'The Nag', Nr. M56 & A56 junction on the Chester Road side of the roundabout. 2nd Tuesday in the month.
Area Reps: Paul Nicholls, David Neill and Chris Walden. Tel: 061436 2121. (AREA 15)
EAST ESSEX: Runwell Hall Hotel, Runwell Road, Wickford, Essex. Last Wednesday in the month.
Area Rep: Nigel Webb, 107 High Street, Shoeburyness, Essex. Tel: Shoeburyness 4231 or Southend-on-Sea 586657. (AREA 16)
NEW YORK (USA): Long Island, New York. First Saturday in the month.
Area Rep: Tom Jaycox, Box 604, Stony Brook 11790, Long Island, New York, USA. (AREA 17)
LANCASHIRE: Lea-Gate Hotel, Blackpool Road, Nr. Preston, Lancs. 1st Thursday in the month.
Area Rep: Steve Freeman, 6 Nookfield, Goosnargh, Preston, Lancs. PR3 2BS (AREA 18)
LEEDS: The Plough, Saxton, Yorks. First Monday in the month.
Area Rep: Malcolm Buckeridge, 306 Undercliffe St., Undercliffe. (AREA 19)
SOUTH WALES: The Coach and Horses, Castleton, Gwent. 1st Thursday in the month.
Area Rep: John Butts, Tredegar Fach, Newbridge, Gwent. Tel: Newbridge 243705. (AREA 20)
BUCKS: The Bricklayers Arms, Lent Rise Road, Burnham, Bucks. 2nd Monday in the month.
Area Rep: Mike Cooper, address as above. (AREA 22)
CHILTERNS: The Bull & Butcher, Turville, Nr. Henley-on-Thames, Oxon. 3rd Monday in the month.
Area Rep: Bob Archard, 31 Amersham Road, High Wycombe, Bucks. Tel: High Wycombe 31557. (AREA 23)
S. SURREY: The Red Lion, Guildford Road, Lightwater, Bagshot. 1st Friday in the month.
Area Rep: Charles Warner, XKUAR, 104 Guildford Road, Lightwater, Bagshot, Surrey. (AREA 26)
CORNISH AREA: Slade House Cottage Hotel, Wadebridge, Cornwall (Wadebridge, Bodmin Road). 3rd Saturday in the month.
Area Reps: John and Sharon James, Sevenside, Betty Adit, Brea, Cornwall. (AREA 27)
N. LONDON: Nuffield Arms, Western Avenue, London. 3rd Wednesday in the month.
Area Rep: Tim Spital, The Cottage, Hill Top Road, London NW6. Tel: 01-624 9360. (AREA 28)
SUFFOLK: Eagle Inn, Sicklesmore (A134), Nr. Bury St. Edmunds, Suffolk. 1st Monday in the month.
Area Rep: E.T. Coleman, Longueville House, Hawksmill Street, Needham Market, Suffolk. Tel: Needham Market 380. (AREA 29)
NORTHERN IRELAND: Homestead Inn, Ballyaughlis, Drumbo, Lisbon, Co. Down. 2nd Monday in the month.
Area Rep: Doug Pearce, 15 Greenwell Street, Newtownards, Co. Down. (AREA 30)
EAST MIDLANDS: The White House, (River Bar), Kegworth (Nr. M1, J24). Third Monday in the month.
Area Rep: John Williams, Ivy Nook, Hamilton Drive, The Park, Notts. Tel: Nottingham 40347. (AREA 31)
S. YORKSHIRE: The Brentwood, Moorgate, Rotherham. 2nd Monday in the month.
Area Rep: Stephen Davies, 23 Grange View Road, Kimberworth, Rotherham, S. Yorks S61 2AQ. Tel: Rotherham 79246. (AREA 32)
NORTH ESSEX: The Kings Arms, Frating (A133) Nr. Colchester, Essex. Second Monday in the month.
Area Rep: Stuart Wright, "Latchetts", 65 Chelmsford Road, Holland-on-Sea, Clacton, Essex CO15 5DJ. Tel: 0255 812057.
NEW YORK CITY GROUP: Tom Burnet and Art Kinnear, 31 Duck Lane, West Islip, N.Y. 11795, USA.
Tel: 358 2864 after 9pm for details of meetings.

OVERSEAS

AUSTRALIA Ian Cummins, 77 Nelson Street, Annandale, NSW 2038, Australia. **BELGIUM** Jacques Gaudfroy, 30 Chemin des deux maisons, Box 9, 1200 Brussels **BRAZIL** W.G. Halberstadt, Rua Haddock Lobo, 281-Apt. o 122, Sao Paulo-Sp-01414 Brazil. **CANADA** Ian Newby, 6362 Chatham Street, West Vancouver, B.C. Canada. **DENMARK** Jens Roder, Lindevej 3A, 3060 Espergaerde, Denmark, Espergaerde 23-40-32 (code from UK 010 453) **FRANCE**.Dr. Phillipe Renault, 39 Avenue de Laumiere, Paris 19, France. **GERMANY** Roger Dunn, Domane Mechtildshausen, 6200 Wiesbaden-Erbenheim. Tel: 06121/73678 **HOLLAND** Evert B. Beket, Astronautenweg 192, 1622 DM. Hoorn. **ITALY** Roberto Causo, Via Condotti 91, 00187 Roma, Italy. Tel: (Home) 8445792 (Business) 6791132/6794003 **NEW ZEALAND** Mr Paul Tavan, P.O. Box 23-139, Papatoetoe, Auckland, New Zealand. **NORWAY** Dag Horne, Tekn. ARVD LFE, Michelets vei 30, 1324 LYSAKER, Norway. **SOUTH AFRICA** Norman Gilmour, P.O. Box 31437, Braamfontein 2017, South Africa **SWEDEN** Bernth Liljegren, Box 42092, 126 12 Stockholm 42, Sweden. **SWITZERLAND** M. Aldo Vinzio, B.P. 34-1211 Geneve 17, Switzerland. **UNITED STATES** Tom Hendricks, 3601, John Carrol Drive, Olney, MD. 20832, U.S.A.

Index to photographs